MONTANA PASSAGE

A HOMESTEADER'S HERITAGE

By Harley Henderson and Lawrence F. Small

Illustrations by Kathleen Wiseman

Publishing Consultant: Falcon Press Publishing Co., Inc., Helena and Billings, Montana

For Arthur and Lulu

Those who labor in the earth are the chosen people of God.

—Thomas Jefferson

TABLE OF CONTENTS

INTRODUCTION

The last great surge to the western frontier occurred early in this century as people from Maine to the Middle Border and abroad took up homesteading in Montana. Few newcomers have been more stereotyped and especially by those who viewed them as intruders upon the Montana scene. Terms like "honyocker" have been used to suggest a rootless, ignorant lot, seeking quick riches but easily duped and robbed of what little they had. Such caricatures ignore the diverse backgrounds of the homesteaders and obscure the fact that their story is a colorful tapestry of many stories, defying simple description. One such story is the subject of this book.

In the one trait homesteaders seemed to have in common, Arthur Henderson was typical. At 23 he was representative of the youthfulness of the Montana migration. Like many, he was of native birth, single, and of farm background. And he came to the promised land by rail. Fortunately, he had relatives waiting to help in filing a claim, so he was spared the enterprising "locator." Like many, he began on a shoestring and faced a long, hard pull in proving up. He was also one of Montana's 6000 homesteaders who served in World War I—in the "Great War," as they called it. With the collapse of the homestead frontier, he was among the determined who weathered the hard years, learning the painful lessons of adjustment and making the necessary changes to become a successful grain grower. His times of hardship and tragedy were not uncommon for Montana pioneers, but they toughened the fibre of character and failed to stay his course. Relatives came and left with the great exodus of the 1920s, but he never seriously considered returning to Kansas. And for him the verdict of the years confirmed the wisdom of his Montana passage.

The Geraldine area in which he located had first caught the eye of stockmen and then the homesteaders. The rolling prairie, interrupted with valleys and draws, was ideal for large herds of cattle and sheep, before the turn of the century brought the tillers of the soil. To the west and south the Highwood range rimmed the region, while the Bear Paws and the Little Rockies stood guard to the east and the north. Square Butte and neighboring Round Butte and little Haystack Butte added something distinctive to the landscape and helped returning travelers to know when they were nearing home. Fort Benton and Great Falls provided markets and access to the world beyond. It was an area that, despite the hard times, rewarded the diligent and the enduring with some of the best grain production in the Northwest.

This book is based upon information gathered by Arthur Henderson's younger brother, Harley, during a visit in the late 1970's. The writers wish to acknowledge sources which have been helpful in the preparation of this manuscript. Especially useful was the publication of the Geraldine Bicentennial Committee, *Spokes, Spurs, and Cockleburs*, River Press Publishing Co., 1976. Also helpful on the Fort Benton area was Joel F. Overholser's *Fort Benton, World's Innermost Post*, River Press, October 22, 1980, and on World War I Chester K. Shore, compiler, *Montana in the Wars*, Miles City, 1977. Appreciation is expressed to Karen Sample for research assistance, to Kathleen Wiseman for the drawings, and to John Willard and Professors Delbert Langbell and Larry Weirather for reading portions and making suggestions on the manuscript. John and Albert Leuthold kindly shared reflections on wheat growing in Montana. Any errors in fact or interpretation remain the responsibility of the writers.

Billings, Montana
Spring 1983

THE WAY OUT

It was cold in the old river town. The thermometer at the depot read 30 below. The new year of 1914 had come in warm and dry, with January one of the mildest in recent memory. But the early days of February brought the first severely cold weather of the winter, blanketing the state and dumping the heaviest snowfall for that month since 1910. Eastern Kansas was seldom like this, and the two young homesteaders just off the warm train sought what comfort they could find in tightly wrapped overcoats, two pairs of cotton gloves, and one-buckle overshoes.

Back in Great Falls, where they changed trains, they had hoped to stretch stiff muscles after the long ride and see the town. But as they got off a piercing north wind whipped snow against their faces, stinging and numbing and making breathing difficult. So they had hurried to the depot to wait for the Great Northern to Fort Benton.

Neither Arthur Henderson nor Bert Bingaman had strayed far from home before their Montana venture. Arthur's main railroad experience had been a trip with his family from Illinois to Kansas in 1907. Like Bert, he was more at home on the back of a horse or a wagon loaded with hay. There were, of course, those times of reckless excitement for the Kansas farm boy, speeding over a dirt road, trailing a cloud of dust, in a buggy or surrey behind a team of spirited horses. But trains were a luxury for young men who seldom had more than a few coins to rattle in their pockets. Occasionally, Arthur and Bert had hopped a freight to husk corn in Iowa or to get to a western Kansas wheat harvest. Buying a ticket was something else. Paying out hard-earned cash for a train ticket was not a country boy's idea of frugality. There had to be a strong urge, the kind of compelling reason that had taken the two young Kansans on their first big adventure.

For several years, relatives and neighbors in eastern Kansas had been uprooting for the last great land of promise in the Northwest. Government pamphlets and railroad promotions pictured a region where nature was kind and ready to reward ambition. Where rainfall was a problem, a benevolent government was introducing irrigation agriculture. One such advertisement scattered widely through the Midwest pictured Uncle Sam holding a sprinkling can, saying, "Uncle Sam is watering a farm for you." Inside the folder listed a wide variety of crops to be grown, with probable yields that were guaranteed to get attention.

Arthur was nearing 23, had been working on the family farm for his room and keep, and was restless to try something different. That urge was in the Henderson blood. His father, Charles Albert or Ab, as he was called, had been born in Kentucky but then moved to Illinois, where he married Mary "Mame" Huckelbridge in 1886. Arthur came along in 1891 on a farm near Bunker Hill. He was the third child and first son in a family that would number eleven children. Ab was well endowed physically for frontier farming. A muscular and agile six feet, he could run and jump and wrestle in a way that won him the respect of friend and foe alike. In contrast to her fully-whiskered husband, Mame was small with delicate features that belied unusual physical endurance. Her people had come from England back in the 1830's to a rugged Illinois frontier where bear were still numerous and sometimes too curious. And old bear tooth on the Huckelbridge mantel was silent testimony to one which tried to invade the still unfinished house.

Arthur came at a time when agrarian unrest was cresting on the farms of the South and West. Farmers were in a losing battle with bankers and railroads, insects and weather, and frustrated by their political powerlessness. Since 1887 drought had plagued the Plains and thousands of farms were reverting to the mortgage companies. Wagons rolled back East with scrawled slogans like "In God we trusted, in Kansas we busted." By 1891, however, the farmers were finding both voice and vote through the Alliance movement and the Peoples or Populist Party. Ab was a Democrat but of the western variety, and he liked what the Populists were saying. It was time to "raise less corn and more Hell." Populists made a good showing in the Election of 1892 with a presidential candidate who received more than 8% of the vote. But they remained too regional, mostly strong in the mountain states, and by 1896 they had lost much of their support to the Democrats and the free silver issue. Ab was solidly behind his party's new crusader, William Jennings Bryan, in the fateful election of that year.

Rising agricultural prices and an improved cycle of weather helped diffuse the farmers' anger and again the West became the place of promise. Ab had been hearing good reports about Kansas and was ready to plant his feet further West. In his several moves, he was a good example of the mobility of life on the frontier. Amy, the oldest girl, had already gone to Kansas to care for her grandparents and to seek relief, she hoped, from encroaching tuberculosis. Also, Ab had two brothers farming near a small frontier town called Richmond. Land was cheap and as fertile as anything in Illinois, so Ab figured it was time to make the move.

One evening in the spring of 1907, after the children had been bedded down, Ab reread a recent letter from Amy and suddenly announced: "Mame, it's going to take a lot of acres for our boys in a few years, so I have been thinking we ought to move to Kansas."

Mame was not surprised, but did point out that they would be leaving all of her people, most of his, and many of their friends. "But," she added, "Amy's health does seem better in Kansas, your brothers are there, and you're restless here. You won't be content until we try our luck further West."

Ab took her response as confirmation and pointed out that he should make plans to leave right away in order to be in Kansas in time for a spring crop. He could go ahead and locate a farm near Richmond and then send for her and the children. Arthur was now a capable seventeen and could see to the loading of all family belongings on the freight car. And so the move was made.

The fabric of life on the Henderson farm in Kansas was woven of toil, the struggles of a large family, the times of joy, and the near brushes with death. Mame taught her daughters the skills of home making and Ab had his sons behind the plow by the age of ten. As the oldest son, Arthur shouldered the main responsibilities in his father's absences. One day, in early spring, the three youngest children, Flossie, Harley, and two-year-old Opal were playing in the yard in a pile of soft warm dirt that sifted between their toes.

Everything was fine until Dewey, a large stock dog with white on his two front feet and a spot between his ears that nearly reached to the tip of his nose, decided to join them. Ab was a strong Democrat and had named the dog for a kindred spirit who ran for a local office. As it turned out, both were losers. For on this particular day, Dewey was acting sick and the children were warned to stay clear of him for fear of rabies.

Flossie and Harley raced to the house, shouting to their mother, who then had to rescue her youngest from the dirt pile. That evening, while the sun hovered in the sky, Arthur came in from work and was at once advised by his mother that Dewey would have to be tied up before he bit one of the children. Bertha, the second oldest, volunteered for the task, but Arthur announced in no uncertain terms that that was his responsibility. Having gotten a rope from the barn, he found Dewey sprawled under a wagon. Already his mouth was covered with foam. Easing under the wagon and speaking softly to the dog, Arthur gently slipped the rope around his neck and secured it to the wagon wheel. Bit by bit he moved backward until he was able to stand up and, breathing easier again, walked back to the house.

It was about dusk when Ab got home and noticed Dewey tied to the wagon. Both Arthur and Claude, who was next in age, had come out to take care of his wagon and he inquired, "Is Dewey worse? I notice you have him tied up." When Arthur replied that he was frothing at the mouth and could be going, mad, Ab nodded in agreement and asked for his shotgun. Presently Dewey was put out of his misery.

Arthur and Claude were close as brothers. Arthur favored his mother and was built small and durable, while Claude was strong and sizeable like his father. On occasion when the boys put on the boxing gloves or decided to wrestle, Arthur was at a distinct disadvantage, but their feelings for each other ran deep and would survive the distances and the years. Less amiable were the relations between younger brothers Cecil and Rolland who found frequent occasion to disagree. When he could manage the time, Ab took his four older sons fishing or hunting in the countryside around Richmond. So they grew up with pleasant memories of a summer afternoon with willow poles and angleworms dangled in a stream or tracking rabbits across a frozen Kansas field.

Music was an important part of the Henderson way of life. Both Ab and Mame played the reed organ and added their voices to the community church choir. They also found time to conduct a singing school. Sunday afternoons the children gathered around their parents for a hymn sing, featuring the stirring salvation songs of the Moody-Sankey variety. Amy, the eldest, was especially musical and gave piano lessons. She and her mother were strongly religious, and Mame held out hope that one day Arthur might want to become a preacher.

It was Amy who often took the younger children to Sunday School, with Charley, the old sorrel horse, hitched to the buggy. The trip was routine and Old Charley could make it half asleep. One day, however, on the way back, something spooked him and he broke into a full gallop. By the time they reached a river crossing the buggy was out of control and flipped over on its side. Charley seemed to sense the danger to his passengers and just as suddenly stopped. Fortunately, it was a dry riverbed, but even so Amy and the children had numerous cuts and bruises.

But Amy's anger with Old Charley was soon forgotten. She had more important things on her mind and was soon announcing that she would be marrying Luther Carter. The Carters had farmed around Richmond for some while, and Luther was well equipped for the task, standing over six feet and weighing a husky 190 pounds. Amy was a replica of her mother and looked more like a child beside him than the wife who would be sharing the rigors of the Montana frontier. Brother Fred Carter had already filed on a homestead in Fort Benton country and Luther and Amy intended to follow him there.

Amy's wedding was just after Christmas in 1909 and a big event for the Henderson clan. From a pattern she found in a catalogue, she designed and made her own wedding dress, purchasing the material at the country store, then cutting, sewing, and fitting while Mame nodded her approval. The Hendersons agreed that it was a thing of notable beauty.

Mame always tried to keep one room for special occasions and guests. It had a carpet on the floor, a rocking chair, even a divan, and, of course, the old reed organ. For the wedding, an archway was fashioned from colored paper, cloth, and limbs from a cedar tree. A touch here and another touch there and the room became a place of wedding splendor. Buggies filled the yard as neighbors and friends shared the moment of solemnity and gladness. Bertha played the organ and the young couple exchanged their vows. It was no hurry up affair. For the Hendersons, weddings were sealed in heaven and marked the beginning of a new generation.

Soon Amy and Luther were filling trunks and boxes and loading a wagon for the trip to the railroad station in Richmond. Their destination was a distant land. Despite letters from friends and relatives, Montana was remote and, for the first time, the family felt the misgivings and the sadness of parting. Not knowing when if ever they would all be together again, Ab made arrangements with a photographer to take a family portrait.

With Amy gone, Bertha viewed anew the prospects of a young woman in her early twenties. She was tall, like her father, slim and energetic, and fun to have around. You could count upon her to enliven the neighborhood parties. Unlike Arthur who was not much for conversation, Bertha tended to keep up a constant chatter. Amy's marriage quickened her interest in suitors, and thoughts of her own wedding and family helped to redeem the monotony of farm life. Dreams of romance broke the bleakness of Monday wash, Tuesday iron, Wednesday bake, Thursday mending of clothes and house cleaning, until the week was gone and you started all over again.

Harold's arrival in 1912 completed the Henderson clan. Remarkably, only one of the eleven children did not survive infancy. Harold came on a school day, and when Harley and Flossie dashed into the house, Bertha took them to their mother's bedroom and showed them their newborn brother. Bertha did her share of the nursing and healing of wounds in the family. When Harley got entangled in some new barbed wire, he ran screaming to the house with blood streaming from his mouth and soaking his shirt. It was too much for Mame. "Bertha," she gasped, "I can't stand it. You take care of him." Beneath the blood and dirt and grime, Bertha found a long deep gash that practically severed Harley's lower lip. Gently she closed the cut, bandaged the lip and changed his clothes. No doctors were called for such emergencies, though perhaps a few stitches would have prevented the ugly scar Harley would carry for the rest of his life.

Hardly less terrifying for little Harley were some of the games the older boys and girls played, especially something called post office. His introduction came on an occasion when as a first grader he was expected to go into a dark room and kiss his teacher. The fact that she was a pretty young woman meant nothing, as he first hid in a corner and then squirmed and wiggled and almost pulled his way to freedom. Finally, a teenage cousin came to the rescue and Harley consented by way of compromise to kissing her. It seemed the only way to get out of his fix. Harley liked parties on the whole, but it would be some years before this game was fully appreciated.

6

Meanwhile, Bertha and a young farmer named Albert [Bert] Bingaman had begun keeping company. They had a lot in common in their enjoyment of life. Bert was jovial and loved to play his guitar and harmonica. He was ambitious, too, and already had a rented farm with cows, horses, chickens, and pigs. Full-faced and clean-shaven, Bert was built like a wrestler and just as strong. He did have a certain awkward way about him, and if it were possible to get a fence in crooked, he could manage it.

One day in the summer of 1912, with little announcement and less ceremony, Bertha and Bert were married by a justice of the peace. Their one concession to the occasion was Bert's black suit and high, stiff collar, and Bertha's long, white dress with pleated bodice, lace neck, and ribbon in her hair. Ab and Mame watched their second daughter pack her few possessions and move to her new home. The Hendersons were frequent visitors there, especially the younger brothers and sisters who liked to while away an evening listening to Bertha play the organ and Bert his harmonica or guitar.

With Amy and Bertha gone, Ab hired a young girl to help with the house. Arthur missed his older sisters and began to ponder his own future. Working for his room and keep put little money in his pockets with which to strike out on his own. One evening after the chores were done, Ab spoke to his three oldest boys about making some money harvesting corn. A neighbor had eighteen acres that needed cutting and was offering a dollar an acre for the job. Arthur commented that he could use some money, and especially in that he and Bert had been talking about homesteading in Montana. Ab professed some surprise at their plans but noted that according to Amy's letters wheat seemed to do better there than in Kansas. Since Arthur was over 21, it might be the thing to do to get his own farm.

Meanwhile, there was corn to be cut. Ab had two corn sleds and his neighbor one and there were enough mules so the boys could get started early. Early meant having the sleds in the field by sunrise. A corn sled was hard work. It was made with two logs nailed together far enough apart so each log would run in the center of a row. The center of the sled would cover a row of corn and as it was pulled forward a long knife attached to one side of a V would automatically cut each corn stock which was held in place by steel rods curved inward at chest level of an average sized man. A man using such a sled had to guide each stock tightly against the curved section until an armload was cut. Then he would lift it off the sled and throw it on the ground directly behind him. The next row would go crosswise on the armload until the corn could be stood straight up into a

7

shock. Generally, sixteen rows would make a corn shock, so the driver would go over eight rows and start again.

With their sleds, Arthur and his brothers started the eighteen acre field at daybreak. Claude and Cecil were both considerably larger than Arthur and could carry heavier loads, but at sunset when the last row was cut and the final corn shock completed each one had managed six acres apiece—a record in those parts. Ab's boys knew the discipline and the value of hard work. And Arthur had his first few dollars to put aside for the Montana journey.

But family misfortune the fall of 1913 would postpone his plans. First, Ab decided to join in a community rabbit hunt which was intended to rid the area of an overabundance of rabbits and add a small fund for community projects. He had just purchased a sixteen gauge repeater shotgun, so if he missed the first shot, he still had five more to go. He was anxious to try it out.

It was a cold and damp autumn day and by evening Ab's legs were soaking wet from walking through tall grass and brush and wading shallow streams. He had started out that morning with a slight cold and by evening was feeling sick enough to skip the celebration and come directly home. He had lost first place to the local doctor in the number of rabbits killed. Ab went to bed where he was to remain for over two months. His cold worsened into pneumonia, the dread disease that claimed so many lives on the frontier. Often he burned with fever and then came a seige of hiccups that wracked his body for three days. Poor Ab was not helped by well-meaning neighbors who fed him sure-fire cures for the hiccups, but which made him vomit and so misery was added to misery. Only a stout constitution and strong will pulled him through.

Later that fall Bertha came home to have her baby. It proved to be a painful birth. Her screams were hard to bear as her flesh was torn apart in the delivery of a ten pound boy. It was three weeks before Bertha could touch her feet to the floor. She had brought her own hired girl, Clara, but Mame was swamped with the care of a sick husband, a new mother and infant, and a family in all of fourteen to feed.

One day, Opal, now four, decided to help Clara with the evening meal. She put some wood in the kitchen range, poured on a liberal supply of kerosene, and lighted a match. Flames flashed to the ceiling and in a second she was on fire. She screamed, jumped down from the chair on which she had been standing to light the fire, and ran toward the parlor where Bertha was wrapped in blankets on the divan. Mame and Clara were in the room and frantically tried to smother the flames engulfing Opal with their hands. Ab lunged from his bed with a blanket and covered the burning child. Soon the flames were out but Opal was burned to the bone.

The doctor did his best in treating the burns, but the pain was so unbearable that only lapses into unconsciousness brought the child any relief. Every day the doctor tended the bandages, and despite the ointment, often pulled flesh when he removed them. As the days passed, Opal would cry whenever she saw his little red car shaped like a buggy with high wheels and small rubber tires drive up to the front gate. Somehow he pulled her through, but it would be years before Opal would not cringe whenever a doctor came by.

It was obvious that Bertha would not be able to travel to Montana for several months. Homesteading for her was out of the question for a while. Under the circumstances, Arthur and Bert decided that they had better go ahead, locate some land, and file their claims. Spring would come soon enough and they would need to have some wheat in the ground. Ab was still weak from his long illness but was getting around and he encouraged Arthur to make his move. He and the other boys could handle things on the farm. "I think you and Bert better get started. By the time you take up your claim, get a team of horses and break a few acres of sod, it will be time to plant."

Money would be the problem. Arthur had not been able to save enough to buy even the wheat seed. Bert had a little cash from the sale of his cows, horses and farm machinery. Ab mentioned that he had been thinking of selling out and relocating in Louisiana. A land agent had been in Richmond promoting virgin land there at a reasonable price. Some of the farmers around Richmond were planning on moving in the spring. Ab reasoned that he might do the same thing, sell his farm and share some of the proceeds with Arthur and with Claude who also wanted to get started on his own place. Arthur gave that possibility some thought but concluded that there would hardly be enough to go around. Besides, he was now anxious to make his move, even if it meant getting started in Montana piecemeal. Ab understood his son's desire and somehow, despite the hard winter and all of the medical bills, found $100 to send him on his way.

Bertha was still convalescing and learning to mother her son who was named for Arthur. She dreaded the thought of separation but agreed that the men should go and get things started. Kissing Bert lightly on the cheek, she whispered, "I'll trust my husband to be away from me for a few months, so run along and make us a cozy little house in Montana." Then drawing him close to her breast, she added, "What's three or four months when compared to a life time on our own farm." Bert agreed as his strong arms held her close in an embrace that would have to last him for quite a while.

Leaving Richmond the last of January, 1914, on the Santa Fe, they trained north to Kansas City and then took the Union Pacific west. There was nothing new in the scenery and neither cared much for reading, so they slept most of the way across Kansas. That seemed to be the best solution for the hard double seats of the old coach and the monotony of the prairie at 35 or 40 miles per hour. Mountain country was something else. The towering peaks rather intimidated the young plainsmen and Arthur began having second thoughts about the journey.

In Wyoming, they looked out on country that was already rich in history. Immemorially old were the Indian paths the mountain men had learned to follow in their never-ending search for beaver water. Oregonians headed west through South Pass to the fertile Willamette Valley had left their deeply rutted trails. Mormons had come this way, pushing their handcarts before them on the way to the New Zion. Here 10,000 Indians of the Plains had met in great council with the white men in a futile effort to live at peace. Here, too, ranchers and rustlers had turned the land into a battle ground. But little of this was known to Arthur and Bert as they watched this new country with growing fascination. Backgrounded by rugged mountain ranges, the pasture lands rose and fell and faded into the distance. Here and there deep depressions rose to pointed ridges and gave the impression of a giant washboard.

Their first break in the long journey came at Huntley Project, an irrigation district near Billings, where Bert's brother, Oliver, was living. The project was on the south side of the Yellowstone River, in a valley that was inhabited when the pharoahs built their pyramids along the Nile. Huntley was one of the first such projects sponsored by the federal government. The land had been a part of the Crow Reservation and Indian labor had been mainly involved in the construction of the ditches. June 26, 1907, had been the red letter day when the Project was officially opened and a special train of notables came down from Billings, including Montana senators Thomas Carter and Joseph Dixon, along with the Secretary of the Interior.

By 1914, most of the initial engineering problems on the Project had been worked through. Unreliable wooden headgates were being replaced by concrete ones and homesteaders who came knowing nothing about irrigating were learning not to flood the roads. The once arid land of sage brush and greasewood was now yielding good crops. Settlers had moved in from all over the country and represented many occupations. Oliver pointed out that the Project included, along with farmers from Iowa and Kansas, former doctors and druggists, lawyers and businessmen, ministers and newspaper editors, ex-professors and shoe salesmen, even a writer for the *Ladies Home Journal*, and an engineer who had worked on the Panama Canal. Business was growing and the first school had been opened in the fall of 1908.

Arthur and Bert enjoyed their visit but were not particularly impressed by the Project. Severe cold weather and heavy snow had moved in and the place seemed too confined, too hemmed in by the rimrocks of the Yellowstone River on the north, and the foothills of the Pryor Mountains on the south. After a three day stay with Oliver, they were anxious to resume their journey and so took the train to Great Falls, and thence to Fort Benton. Whatever else they were to learn about this new land, they knew it could be cold.

THE HOMESTEADERS

There was little to suggest to the young Kansans the rich history of this old river town. It seemed rather forlorn in winter's grip on that February morning of 1914, guarded by high cliffs of sandstone and clay. Gone were the steamboats from the levee, unloading their freight from St. Louis, Yankton, or Sioux City—or taking on furs, buffalo robes, gold and silver bullion, wool, cattle, or sheep for the trip down stream. For local residents the arrival of a paddle-wheeler had stirred excitement and anticipation. Would the cargo include one's supplies ordered from St. Louis? Fresh fruit was always high on the list of desirables, as a welcome relief from munching on white turnips called "Montana apples."

1879 had been the peak year for river traffic with 47 boats arriving—and then the railroads came. In 1883, the Canadian Pacific reached Calgary, dooming trade to the north, and the Northern Pacific connected at Gold Creek. By September of 1887, when Mrs. James J. Hill drove the silver spike at Benton, the great days of steamboating on the Upper Missouri were indeed gone.

Gone, too, with the river trade were the bull trains and mule trains and stage lines that fingered out from Fort Benton in all directions. The ponderous bull trains of 24 to 30 wagons sometimes carrying cargoes of 200,000 pounds and more crawled across the prairie to the gold camps and other points and north to Canada, the oxen urged on by the bullwhacker's talented whip and by the unrestrained language of the plains. The mule trains carried "fast freight" but were more expensive, and the 'skinners tended to be a prideful lot, imagining themselves as the cream of the crop of freighters.

Gone was the rich mix of humanity that crowded the wharves, the dusty streets, and the numerous saloons. The editor of the *New Northwest* at Deer Lodge found in Benton "all the exuberant array of the American frontier"—lumbermen from Minnesota, farmers from all over, French-Canadian rivermen, greedy whiskey traders, fringed fur traders, soldiers, miners from the west, desperadoes, clergymen, speculators, land seekers, government officials, and the stiff-collared merchants hurrying through the streets to their prosperous establishments. Two or three of the last had become merchant princes with inland empires of commerce, receiving and sending goods from all corners of the land—and beyond. Fort Benton had thrived as the trading hub of the region until the mid-eighties when the railroads and rival Great Falls helped to usher in harder times. A local historian would speak later of the 1890's as the "drab decade".

But, meanwhile, the same historian found in 1882, the "greatest year" for Fort Benton. Construction of new buildings was at a peak, and most notable was the opening of the 60 room Grand Union Hotel on November 1. Three stories of the best in accommodations, it provided female guests with a separate entrance, stairway, and parlors so that they would not have to mingle with the rough patrons. With furnishings of the finest in woods and velvets, the Grand Union was second to none in the Northwest. The formal opening topped all other social events in the town's colorful history. The lobby of the Grand Union with its glistening chandeliers offered a warm welcome to tired travelers of the northern plains. Cowboys bone-weary from the fall roundup or after endless hours in a line shack were more than ready for a hot bath, clean linens, and one of the hotel's famous meals. Christmas was always a big occasion with the Grand Union featuring an elaborate bill of fare guaranteed to delight the most fastidious gourmet with such goodies as canape of Russian caviar, lobster a la Newberg, stuffed young Montana turkey, roast suckling pig, steamed English and Yorkshire puddings and so on. But the Grand Union all too soon became the symbol of a prosperity that was passing. In 1899, it was sold for a fraction of its construction costs.

Census figures told the decline of the river town: 1618 in 1880, 624 in 1890, 1024 in 1900, 1004 in 1910. It would not be until mid-way through the new century that Fort Benton would match again the population of 1880. Meanwhile, Great Falls with Paris Gibson's leadership was growing rapidly and by 1910 could boast a population of 13,948, second only to Butte with 39,165. Chouteau County itself experienced a notable growth with 4741 in 1890, 10,966 in 1900, 17,191 in 1910. Numerous little farming centers with their grain elevators began to dot the county. Population more than kept pace with that of the state which was 142,924 in 1890, and 376,053 in 1910.

Arthur and Bert came to Benton country during the last great days of the homestead frontier. It was the final phase of a centuries-old westering migration that goes deep in the meaning of American history, that, leaving the Atlantic shore, was held back for some while by the Appalachians before it poured through the mountain passes into the lake plains and gulf plains regions and thence across the broad Mississippi and up the Missouri. The mounting pressures for free land on the frontier failed to move a Congress badly split between North and South, until 1862, the men of the Union were free to pass the Homestead Act. It changed the way of life for millions of Americans in providing for 160 acres of the public domain for a $10 filing fee and a five-year commitment to "proving up"

Yet, the Homestead Act held problems and disappointments for the land seekers. Foremost was the fact that 160 acres made little sense in the semi-arid spaces of the Great Plains, in a hostile environment demanding radical adaptation in farming methods and attitudes toward life. Subsequent land legislation was of limited benefit to the average homesteader. The Timber Culture Act of 1873 offered 160 acres if the owner would plant at least one fourth of the land to trees within four years. There were some 65,000 takers during the fifteen years the law was in existence. The Desert Land Act of March, 1877, sold 640 acres at $1.25 an acre to the homesteader who would irrigate them. Ranchers more than farmers found ingenious ways to get the most out of this legislation. Of greater assistance was the Enlarged Homestead Act of 1909, which offered free a 320 acre half-section, and which was supplemented by the Three-Year Homestead Act of 1912, limiting the "proving up" period to three years. Additionally, the settler could be absent from his land for five months of each year.

Some 300,000 land-seekers had responded to the initial legislation before the end of the Civil War. Then came the first surge, and the population of the trans-Mississippi West soared from under 7 million in 1870 to nearly 17 million in 1890. Yet even more land was homesteaded after 1900. In Montana, the boom years were from 1910 to 1918, when some 32 million acres were taken up. Chouteau County in 1880 had something over 80 farms, mostly in the Highwood country, but it started to fill up fast after 1910. By then the newcomers were crowding the cattle outfits.

For a man of vision like Paris Gibson, growing up in Brownfield, Maine, in a region of rocky soil and limited harvests, the rolling high plains offered boundless opportunity. Not every one could be a cattle or sheep baron or a copper king nor should they apologize for tilling the soil. They had Thomas Jefferson's word for the worth and dignity of their work. "While we have land to labor," the great Virginian had proclaimed, "let us never wish to see our citizens occupied at a work bench, or twirling a distaff, for those who labor in the earth are the chosen people of God."

The generous years following 1910 saw ample rainfull and the elevators filling with good grain crops. Statewide in 1912 the wheat harvest brought in 25 million bushels, representing a four-fold increase since 1909. 1914 was an excellent year in Chouteau County, with wheat selling at 90 cents a bushel. And the coming of the war would send prices sharply upward. Most of the good land in the county was gone by then, so that Arthur and Bert were fortunate to have relatives on the scene. They were much better off than many new arrivals in that regard in not needing to pay for the services of a locator. For a fee that ranged from $20 to $50 this enterprising gent took the homesteader in his wagon and helped him find and file on a piece of land. Since he frequently had land to sell, more desirable than any to be found, he worked that angle and often made a sale. The locator met the incoming trains and sometimes serviced several land seekers in a single day. It was a profitable business while it lasted.

Unlike many homesteaders, Arthur and Bert had also traveled light, unencumbered by household possessions. Arthur had Ab's gift of $100 and a dream. Bert did not have much more. But if they would have to start from scratch, at least they had been spared the trials of the immigrant car. By that arrangement, the homesteader could rent a freight car and jam it with all of his worldly goods, household articles, farm implements and vehicles, grain, trees, shrubbery, and limited numbers of hogs, sheep, horses, chickens, mules, and cattle. At times, in the midst of all else, a grand piano or reed organ would be transported across the plains. If livestock were included, the owner could ride free and he often smuggled in an older son to help him. More than one young man would retain memories of long days and nights in a slowly moving, smelly immigrant car or, even worse, sitting in a freight yard waiting for the livestock to be inspected and vaccinated before crossing state lines. The fee from St. Paul to Montana points was $50, while the rest of the family in the passenger coach paid a special homesteader's rate of $12.50.

Homesteaders, of course, were not all farmers, like Arthur and Bert. Many had been enticed by railroad promotions away from bench and desk and class room to Jim Hill's golden land of opportunity. Most were native born, though there were generous numbers of Germans and Scandinavians and others. And the majority were young, like Arthur and Bert, in their twenties or early thirties. So our two Kansans were a part of one of the great migrations of American history as they made their way from the depot to catch the stage to Geraldine.

The stage proved to be a spring wagon entirely open to snow and cold. The driver, though, looked warm enough in his heavy sheeplined coat and fur mittens. "Where are you from?" he inquired in a friendly way of his two passengers. "Kansas," Arthur replied, as he eyed the horses admiringly. "You must be a farm boy the way you're sizen up my team." "Yes," Arthur nodded, as he began to find this first contact with Montana more and more to his liking. "What do you fellas plan to do here?" the driver continued. "We hope to file on a claim. My sister and her husband live a few miles from Geraldine. Bert and I intend to stay with them until we can get settled."

"Oh," the driver's interest quickened, "what's your sister's name? I know most of the settlers in these parts." Arthur ventured his brother-in-law's name. "'Luke Carter!" the driver beamed a frosty grin, "I know him well. He's one of the finest fellas around here. His brother Fred lives three quarters of a mile or so from my stage route. If you'd like to get off there, it would be a lot closer than trying to find Luke's place in this weather. You could spend the night and Fred could take you tomorrow in his sled."

"That sounds fine," Arthur agreed. "We're not dressed for this Montana weather and three quarters of a mile will be plenty." So they loaded on the trunks and headed out toward Geraldine.

The Carter place was about 16 miles from Fort Benton and midway to Geraldine. Fred Carter had homesteaded there in the spring of 1911 and by the following year had a sizeable house of three rooms, kitchen, bedroom and frontroom. It was a convenient stopping off place for travelers in and out of Benton for supplies and often they spent the night. Many mornings bed rolls would nearly cover the kitchen floor. Latecomers would have to sleep in the barn. There was no need to leave hungry, as breakfast included oatmeal, bacon and eggs, cream biscuits and gravy. Such openhanded hospitality was given and received with the unspoken understanding that pioneers needed one another.

Once off the stage and numbed to the bone, Arthur and Bert set a quick pace to the Carter ranch. There in the warmth of home and friendship, around the dinner table, talk flowed of the old days in Richmond, and for the first time since he had left Kansas, Arthur began to feel a little at peace in this new land. Fred was relieved to hear that his father's health was holding up despite advanced years. The Carters wanted them to spend the night, but Arthur was anxious to go on to Amy's place which was another two and a half miles. So Fred's brother-in-law, Charlie Falls, another Kansas man, hitched up a team to a sled and took them on to their destination.

Amy wept unashamed as she hugged her brother and Arthur struggled with his own tears. It had been four years and they had been close back home. The weariness and the misgivings of the long journey suddenly vanished in the gladness of reunion. Arthur remembered to introduce Bert, and Amy commented that she was anxious to have Bertha around. The isolation of homestead life made for lonely times, especially when you had been raised in a large family. Neighbors were kind but few and far between. For women left with the children for long periods, the yip - yip of prairie dogs by day and the howling of coyotes by night accentuated the loneliness. Yes, how good it would be to have Bertha near! Bert confessed how much he missed her, and then added that he must find some land and build a cabin as soon as possible.

After supper and around the kerosene lamp, they visited about home way into the evening. Arthur's presence revived old memories and Amy had endless questions to be answered. She had not seen the youngest brother, Harold. Who did he favor? Amy was expecting their first child and here Bertha already had little Arthur. Who did he look like? That night, as the heat lingered in the two-hole monkey stove, the two weary travelers slept soundly in their blankets on the cabin floor, each content in the thought that if Luther could build a house and start a farm they ought to be able to do the same.

The plan was for Arthur and Bert to help Luke around the place, removing rocks and preparing a few more acres for planting. Nothing much could be done about locating claims until the weather cleared. They remained for about a month, until the first of March, when a chinook blew in from the Southwest and filled the lakes with melting snow. The rest of the month stayed unusually mild, and the young Kansans got their first taste of Montana as the land of extremes.

Bert's situation was more urgent, and he was anxious to get started. He had a family to think about. Arthur, too, wanted to get a claim filed but he knew that he would have to spend considerable time working around for wages before he could do much with a homestead. At the going rate of $40 a month it would take a while.

Luke advised that there was no government land near his place but that a few miles east of Geraldine you could still get a large piece of flat land with only a few gullies. "As you know," he observed, "this country has rich soil formed by glacier deposits—along with millions of rocks and gullies cutting this way and that."

The gullies, Bert thought, would make good pasture land. Luke agreed but advised that they look for as much flat land as possible. It was unlikely, he added, that they would find adjoining homesteads. Arthur didn't expect that they would but hoped that their claims would be near enough so they could help each other.

Early on the day selected, Amy prepared a solid breakfast and then packed a lunch for the three men. She added some flour, eggs, and a jar of milk with the thought that if they didn't get back by nightfall, they could shoot a rabbit and have some biscuits and gravy for supper. First they wagoned over to Geraldine to get a map showing land that was still available for homesteading. With Luke's guidance, they skirted the marginal areas and looked for fertile soil with a minimum of gullies. Here and there unpainted shacks evidenced a claim and broke the monotony of the seemingly endless land. Arthur was driving and was trying to imagine fields of wheat and cattle grazing on the hillsides. Finally he pulled up at the end of a section that appeared comparatively level, except for a depression near its border.

"Fellas, I think we've gone far enough for me. There's probably 200 acres or more of level land here and that coulee will make good pasture. We can't get beat too bad because it won't cost us anything except hard work." Luke and Bert agreed.

A mile further on they found another homestead of 320 acres, and then rode over to the nearest land office in Square Butte to file their claims. Luke pointed with satisfaction to the evidences of growth in the new farming community. There was the new drugstore and restaurant and pool hall, the Milwaukee depot nearing completion, the livery barn on Front Street, a public hall under construction, and, of course, the spacious grain elevator. This southeastern corner of the county seemed headed for prosperous times, and Arthur and Bert felt good about being there. It had been a full and satisfying day when they got back home—tired, happy, and ready for the supper table.

The next order of business was to find some transportation, as the prairie was a poor place to be on foot. And, later, horses would be needed to pull plows. So Arthur and Bert borrowed Luke's buckboard and rode over to Geraldine to see what might be available. A retired stage driver had a motley bunch of animals—broken down stage horses, old saddle horses, mules, but also some younger ones, including a raven black three-year old that caught Arthur's eye. He was wild but had the makings of a good saddle horse. He gentled down quickly after Arthur broke him, with some help from Luke. "Buster" cost $25 and proved to be durable for the next 25 years. It took courage to pay out another $40 for a secondhand saddle and bridle when you were getting down to your last dollar but Arthur had no choice. He was also counting on Luke's assurances that he could soon find work on a farm.

Bert's finances were somewhat sounder and he invested in a team of horses, wagon, and a cow. He also bought some lumber at one of Geraldine's flourishing lumber yards to get a start on his cabin. While Arthur headed back to Luke's place to return the buckboard and spend the night, Bert drove over to the homestead. Somehow the sun seemed brighter and the plains more alive with the sights and smells of approaching spring as he thought about tomorrow and getting started on his cabin. For the first time, he could turn the sod of his own land, and he and Bertha would have their own home. That night there was not much sleep as in restless anticipation he waited for the first light.

By the time Arthur arrived, Bert had located a spring, sufficient, he thought, for the house and livestock and had also coaxed a pan of milk from the cow. The cabin needed some sturdy poles for the framework and Bert had heard that the nearest place to find them was a mountain called "Square Butte." It was about a day's drive round trip and Arthur volunteered for the job. While he was away Bert could firm up his plans for the cabin, corral, hopefully a well, and whatever else would have to be done.

It was hard to miss Square Butte. This unique elevation rising some 1700 feet above the surrounding plains dominated the landscape of southeastern Chouteau County and looked out over the

Judith Basin. Neighboring Round Butte and modest little Haystack Butte added variety. Long a landmark [Lewis and Clark mentioned it in 1805], Square Butte could be seen for 100 miles around. It was for many returning travelers the symbol of home. On its upper slopes and flat top could be found scattered timber, including tall, slender pines ideal for the framework of the homesteader's cabin and also for making corrals.

Arthur soon had a wagon load and returned home by early evening. Bert had found some boulders flat enough for a foundation and was ready to begin construction in the morning. In a surprisingly short time, the shack became a 12 by 14 reality. There were cracks in the walls where the rough-cut lumber didn't meet, but old newspapers, rags, and tarpaper outside would take care of that. Rough slabs were used to cover cracks in the peaked roof, which would suffice if it didn't rain too hard. A window and a door completed the Bingaman domicile.

Homestead housing varied considerably with available resources. It was not unknown for a family to arrive virtually penniless and spend the first year in a dwelling dug out of the hillside. If they were in luck, the winter would be mild and the friendly banker who shared their optimism for the future would loan them $100 survival money to get through until spring.

Some homesteaders in the area followed the practice of the Nebraska frontier and cut heavy sod for building walls. Roofs varied but a deluxe job consisted of poles close together supporting a layer of flax straw, then heavy roofing paper, topped by sod which served as a kind of shingle. With roughcut lumber for the floor, a window, and a poorly hung door, the sod shanty was ready for occupancy. If it was warm in the winter and cool in the summer, it was also always dirty and a potential disaster when it rained heavily. If fortunate, the owner could count on his dwelling lasting ten years. By then presumably prosperity would have made possible a more spacious and durable frame house.

Most Montanans, like Bert, built wood shanties and achieved some variety in roof style. Some were peaked, others slanted one way, and still others used the box-car roof. This last was quite popular in Geraldine country as it was cheap and durable. A sizeable beam was laid through the center of the roof from end to end, with ship lap bent over it and nailed securely to the plates. Heavy roofing paper completed the job. More established homesteaders, like the Fred Carters, could boast frame houses of three rooms and more.

Homestead shacks were seldom finished inside. Partitions might be no more than blankets hung from the roof or, at best, walls that did not reach all the way up. To utilize every available inch of space, beds were hinged and folded against the wall during the day and were also ideal breeding places for bed bugs. Crates and boxes were converted with some ingenuity into chairs and cupboards. A root cellar beneath the floor or outside provided a place for storing vegetables.

Water was a major problem. The homesteader with a good well had a prized possession and shared his blessing with relatives and neighbors for miles around. Many had to haul water long distances and also build cisterns to trap the rain. Bad water added its curse to the dread diseases of the plains. Typhoid and cholera along with scarlet fever, pneumonia, and small pox left many families in recurrent bereavement.

So with the barest of essentials the Montana homesteader staked out his claim on a new way of life. Amidst the drabbest of surroundings, he dreamed of "making out" and "getting ahead". In the winter a pot-bellied stove provided the margin of survival as snow piled up around the shack and frost accumulated inside and families dug deep beneath quilts and blankets to stay warm. In sub-zero weather it was not uncommon for valuable farm animals to share the cramped space inside. When the wood pile ran out, fence posts were sometimes used. Fortunately, for the homesteaders around Geraldine there was stripmine coal available to be dug. And most of them did.

Summer was also hard on the wife with its stifling heat and winds blanketing the shack with dust, texturing the skin like rough leather, but at least she had her man at home. Winter was the grim time when he had to be away seeking employment. If that lessened the dread of frequent pregnancies, it also left the mother alone with the children in the struggle for survival. Little wonder that the homestead wife aged prematurely, or went to an early grave.

Bert's thoughts, however, were all upbeat as he surveyed their handiwork with a none-too-critical eye and then announced that he was going to Geraldine to send for Bertha. Arthur reminded him to take the wagon and bring back a bed, stove, and lots of pasteboard boxes. The walls definitely needed further attention, and perhaps some clay and pasteboard would do wonders for them. Bert agreed and added that he had better get some more lumber for a table.

Bertha squealed like a delighted teenager when she read Bert's telegram. She was staying with Mame and the younger children on a little farm outside Richmond. Ab's restless spirit had prevailed again and he and Claude had gone to Louisiana to find new acreage. Cecil was working for a neighbor. Bertha was now strong enough to make the trip and face the rigors of homesteading. So without further delay she sent a letter to Bert advising him of her arrival time on the Milwaukee in Geraldine.

For too long Bert had yearned to have Bertha in his arms and she returned the ardor of his embrace. Then there was little Arthur to be hugged. Bert's normally jovial countenance radiated complete happiness as he loaded the wagon and turned the team toward their new home. Bertha noticed homestead cabins along the way and was curious. "Does everyone live in a house as small as the ones we are seeing along this trail?" Bert hedged his reply in observing that the house had to be built small and sturdy to withstand strong winds. Bertha snuggled closer on the seat, planted a kiss on Bert's cheek, and said: "I see. You're trying to tell me our house is little and ugly but firmly anchored to Montana soil. It's all right, lover boy. I'll be happy just to have a place of our own. We can improve on it later."

Arthur had gone back to Luke's and Amy's for a few more days before beginning his own cabin, but was on hand to greet Bertha. Swinging a pail half-full of milk, he walked over to the corral and gave her a big hug. "Did that old cow give that much milk?" she gushed in happiness. "She's not that old," Arthur laughed, "and besides there's a calf that slips around to take about half of what she has. There'll be plenty for little Arthur and some to spare. We may not have all the conveniences, Sis, but we make out all right around the dinner table."

"Well, let's go inside," Bertha said, casting a suspicious glance at the cabin, "and see how many conveniences are packed away in such a small space." As she opened the door, there was a moment of silence, and then an instinctive "oh" as she viewed the bareness within. "It's nice and cozy," she offered in an unsuccessful effort to conceal disappointment, "but it would look better with some kind of shelves for dishes and a place to hang clothes."

Bert assured her that there were plenty of wooden boxes and crates to be had that would make good cupboards and a clothes closet. That would be his next project. Bertha wondered where he would put them. "This shack must be all of 12 by 14." Then she eyed the stove and exclaimed, "How in heaven's name do you bake on anything that little?" "It makes good biscuits," Bert countered, his spirit undiminished. "All you do is put a lid on that heavy iron skillet and they pop right up. And I bet you could make a cake without any trouble. It sure makes good rabbit stew and is just perfect for boiling beans." Then he added, "They make a drum oven that fits on the stove pipe. Fred Carter has one and his wife bakes bread and ducks just fine in it. Someday we can get one."

Bertha obviously had reservations, but the boyish enthusiasm of her young husband was contagious. Pulling him close, running her fingers through his coarse auburn hair, she whispered, "Don't worry, Bert. I'll be just as good a pioneer as you or Arthur. This place is a start and we are together. That's what counts. We have a lifetime to work on a better roof above our heads." With that she announced that she was ready to get her first meal, while Bert could find his guitar and supply some music she had been waiting so long to hear.

Arthur couldn't have been happier as he got Buster from the corral and rode back to Amy's and Luke's. The move to Montana seemed right and full of promise. Bert and Bertha would do well on their place. They were both ambitious and not afraid of hard work. Now he had his own cabin to think about. Luke soon offered to take some time and help him with the project. They obtained poles from Square Butte, found some wide clapboard lumber with groves in Geraldine and shortly had Arthur's cabin well along. The roof slanted one way and completed the 12 by 14 structure. It would be comfortable enough for the young bachelor who would be spending much of his time working for other people.

His first job was helping Tom Dines with his plow. Tom had a heavy steam engine which he used to pull several plows at a time and he needed someone to tend them, to prevent the plows from digging too deeply into the soft dirt or hardly breaking the surface in the hard spots. The pay was $40 a month, but the work was not steady and Arthur had time to wrestle rocks and break sod on his own homestead. Also, that first year he made a deal with a neighbor to plow up what he could not get done of the required forty acres in exchange for the wheat crop.

Spring warmed into summer and with the planting over Arthur hired on with John Jacoby who owned a ranch near Highwood. John had struggled to build his own place and could sympathize with young people just making a start in this new country. He needed a good ranch hand and was willing to arrange Arthur's work so that he could put in the required time on his homestead.

The long awaited event for Amy and Luther came on August 26th with the birth of Mary Amy Carter, named for her maternal grandmother. Bertha was on hand to help the doctor with the delivery. Fall was favorable weatherwise and brought a fair wheat harvest. At

90 cents a bushel, Bert managed to lay by enough money for some flour and seed for the spring planting. By agreement, Arthur's first crop went to his neighbor for doing most of the plowing and planting. As winter closed in, the young Kansans had a feeling of considerable accomplishment since that early February day in Fort Benton when they had first experienced Montana's cold.

BROKEN DREAMS

Winter reinforced the unpredictability of Montana weather. November was abnormally warm, but December was generally exceptionally cold. With the first hint of spring, Arthur was ready to tackle building a corral and needed some more poles from Square Butte. Bert offered to help and early one morning they set out with two wagons, four horses, and enough food to tide them over to the next day. By evening the trees had been cut, trimmed, and loaded, and the weary men were ready for some hot stew. Then wrapped in heavy blankets, they slept soundly with their feet warmed by the campfire.

Bert stirred first with the morning light, stretching his powerful arms and then nudging Arthur. "If you get the breakfast, I'll take care of the horses and maybe we can get an early start home. I imagine Bertha is a little lonesome staying all by herself."

"Sounds good to me," Arthur yawned as he rolled over. "I'm sorta anxious to get started because we could break something on these rough trails."

The two men worked steadily and efficiently to complete their tasks and were soon ready to roll. The poles were firmly tied down and Arthur went for the lead team. Suddenly he stopped. Bert's wagon creaked and he turned quickly to see the heavy load shoving the team forward. Bert reached for a rope attached to the brake pole just as the front wheel hit a chuckhole, knocking him off balance. He grabbed for something to check his fall and missed. As he slid down between the horses, they panicked and pulled the wagon forward. A front wheel hit Bert and crushed him to the frozen ground, rolling over the lower part of his back. Then came the back wheel adding another terrible crunch. The horses, unable to control the heavy load, turned into a coulee. Arthur ran over to Bert who was still conscious but groaning in excrutiating pain.

"Bert, can you move?"

"My legs are dead," he moaned, "and the pain is terrible. I think my back must be broken." Gently Arthur loosened Bert's coat. "I think I better go for a doctor. I'm afraid to move you for fear I'll pull something out of place. I don't see much blood so you're probably bleeding on the inside and need a doctor as soon as possible. Can you hang on while I go for help?"

"Go ahead," he gasped. "I seem to be all right in my chest but the slightest move kills me. My nerves are probably mashed out of shape."

"I'll be back as soon as I can," Arthur assured him as he ran to unhitch Buster. He hated to leave Bert in such misery, but a broken back was far beyond his medical experience. He would have to trust in his brother-in-law's strength to keep alive and pray that a doctor was available in Square Butte.

Arthur raced his young horse over the rugged miles until the powerful legs began to weaken and the last distance into town was made on sheer unyielding spirit. The people in Square Butte knew something was tragically wrong when they saw Arthur riding bareback with a work bridle on an exhausted horse covered with foam. He leaped to the ground and, when he found there was no doctor in town, asked for a volunteer to ride to Geraldine and for somemeone else to get Bertha. Ben LaVanway who had homesteaded nearby in 1909 happened to be at the trading post and offered to go for Bertha. Arthur then located a spring wagon, blankets, and a man to return with him to the mountain.

They found Bert as Arthur had left him, still alive, but in great agony. "I couldn't find a doctor in Square Butte, Bert, but I have a spring wagon and a fella to help me. We'll have to take you to town and probably catch a train to Great Falls."

By this time, Bert was so weak from his long hours of suffering that he mumbled, "Do what you have to, Arthur. Don't mind my yelling." The men quickly fashioned a makeshift stretcher out of the blankets and lifted Bert into the wagon. The pain was more than he could bear and with a loud groan he lapsed into unconsciousness, sparing him the agony of the rough ride to Square Butte.

Both Bertha and a doctor were at the depot. No stranger to tragedy, she kept control of the panic that whelmed within. Her husband lay between life and death, but she knew no amount of hysteria would make him whole. As calmly as she could, she waited for the doctor's examination and then his words: "I can't do anything for him here. We'll have to take him to Great Falls."

That meant longer agonizing hours as the next train from Lewistown through Square Butte was not until tomorrow. It was an interminable night of waiting, as Arthur and Bertha took turns rubbing Bert's legs to keep the blood circulating. That seemed to help ease the pain. Throughout the anxious vigil in the depot, Bert drifted in and out of consciousness. Finally, daylight came and then the train that offered the narrow margin of survival for their loved one.

At the hospital in Great Falls, Bert was rushed into surgery and then came another ordeal of waiting. Arthur tried to comfort Bertha with reassurances about Bert's youth and rugged constitution. But the doctor's words were very guarded. "I don't want to alarm you, but your husband has a broken back. We put it in place the best we knew how and bound him securely. What happens now is in the hands of God and the regenerative powers of nature."

"Thank you, doctor," Bertha answered softly. "May I see him now?" "You most certainly can, but it will be an hour or so before he regains consciousness." She used that time to go to the depot and send a telegram to her father. Throughout her life he had symbolized strength and stability and she knew that she desperately needed him now.

Back in the hospital room, she sat beside her husband, now so pale and quiet and helpless. She struggled with her tears as she thought of the robust young farmer who had wooed her with his guitar and lighted up her life with his love. Finally Bert opened his eyes and she gently caressed his brow and then softly touched her lips to his. That touch brought a glimmer of gladness to eyes long since glazed with pain. His Bertha was here and somehow there would be healing in her presence. His lips moved. "I sorta let you down, honey," he whispered.

"Don't try to talk," she said soothingly, caressing his cheek. "Everything will be all right. We have lots of years to build our home and plant crops." Bert managed a faint smile, and consoled by her presence, slipped back into sleep. Bertha lingered by his bedside, reluctant to leave, as though perhaps somehow in her yearning she could help make him whole again.

Arthur seldom went home during those first critical days but ministered to Bert's every need in an effort to make life a little more bearable for the man who had been like another brother to him. But as the days went by it became obvious that Bert's legs were gone. Slowly the feeling left them, and mercifully, the pain. The future looked grim.

Ab happened to be home when the telegram came. He had been in Louisiana buying a farm and was preparing to return in a few days. Mame read Bertha's message and said without hesitation, "Ab, you'll have to go. If Bert has a broken back, he can't live long. Bertha is not strong enough to take care of a new claim and baby, with or without an invalid husband."

"Yes, I know," he nodded. "I'll take the first train to Great Falls."

When Ab got off the train, he inquired about the location of the hospital. In response to questions, he mentioned his son-in-law having a broken back. Thereupon a cowboy took off his broad-brimmed hat and passed it around the depot. Miners, cowboys, settlers, drummers, travelers generally threw in some money. Obviously, it wouldn't meet the hospital bill, but it would help with immediate expenses and it said something about how people felt. Misfortune was not uncommon on the frontier and such tragedy as had befallen the young couple evoked genuine sympathy and concern. When the cowboy counted the offering, there were forty dollars to be turned over to Ab.

Bert was awake when Ab walked into his room and greeted him with a faint smile. Here was a bit of Richmond and old times along with a caring father-in-law. "It looks like you tackled the wrong fellow", Ab offered in an effort to ease into conversation. "Yeah, I got a little careless. I'd have been all right if that chuckhole hadn't been there, but it was, and I'm here."

Ab asked the obvious question as he held Bert's hand, "How do you feel?"

"Not too bad as long as I lay still, but the least twist or movement seems to pinch smashed nerves and it really kills me." Bert paused and then added, "What worries me most is how to get a field of wheat planted lying in this bed. We'll sure need a good crop after this siege in the hospital."

"Oh, I wouldn't worry much about wheat," Ab replied with the air of one who had lived with disappointment. "One poor crop doesn't make that much difference over a period of years. Just keep your chin up and get out of here as soon as possible."

Ab didn't stay long. He would be visiting Bert again, and he was anxious to talk with the doctors about his son-in-law's chances of survival. They could give him no assurances. Bert's back was crushed beyond repair. It was difficult to predict the outcome of a strong and courageous young man.

Ab found Bertha clinging to the hope that Bert would make it and was anxious to show him where they lived. He, too, wanted to see the places chosen by his children and evaluate Bertha's chances of retaining her claim in the event Bert did not recover or remained an invalid. He also planned to spend a few days helping Arthur, who was swamped with work in trying to care for both homesteads.

As father and daughter rode toward her claim, he said quietly, "As I understand the doctors, Bert may never walk again." He paused before adding, "You better face things as they are, bleak as they may be, and give some thought to your future with or without Bert."

"I know, Papa [she retained the childhood name for him]. Right now Bert thinks he will get well, but the doctors are not encouraging. Whatever happens, though, I want to stay here—whether Bert is back on our homestead or . . . in his grave."

"Is there any work you can get here?" Ab asked, thinking that his daughter would be better off back in Kansas. "You know you have a baby to think about."

"Some of the settlers keep a hired girl so they can spend more time in the field. I can do some work on our claim and also work out—at least, during the winter. The people around here are very good because they are all trying to make a go of it and many of them have experienced some kind of tragedy."

"Yes, I know," Ab nodded. "I saw the kind of friendship and unselfish concern that people around here have when I got off the train. Their generosity in the depot seemed straight from the heart." He paused and then added, "The question is whether you will want to prove up on your homestead in the event Bert is crippled for life or—doesn't make it."

"I don't really know, Papa. It's all so sudden and confusing, but I do know how much it means to me that you are here." That seemed to settle the subject for the while, and they rode on in the comfort of each other's presence to the homestead.

Ab noted with a heavy heart the little prairie shack his daughter called home and how much needed to be done to improve the place. How much better off she would be back in Kansas where he and

Mame could help share her sorrow, but if this is where she wanted to stay, he would do his best the next several days to help around the homestead. Each visit to the hospital found Bert looking more pale and haggard and the light of hope fading from his eyes. Lack of circulation in his lower limbs caused proud flesh and an unpleasant order. It had obviously become just a question of time. The doctors could not say how long, which left Ab torn between staying with Bertha to the end or returning home to pressing duties.

Finally, he told Bertha that he would have to leave, knowing that Arthur and Amy would be near. When he got back to Richmond, he would arrange to send some money to her. "I'm so glad you came, Papa," she whispered appreciatively as she hugged him, "you'll never know how much it has meant to have you here." She had seen her father bury a baby and return home to milk the cows, feed the pigs, and take care of the horses. "I know that life does go on and, if I lose Bert, I'll make out somehow."

Bert lingered for another month. One day, towards the end, he looked longingly at the young wife by his bedside. "Our dreams didn't all come true, but we've had one another. We've shared a love that many never find however long they live. We have our son and . . . I cannot really die because I'm alive in him."

Bertha bent to kiss the drawn lips, somehow now calm in her resignation. "There's another world, we know, and someday we'll both be together again. You had to wait for me a little while here in Montana—you'll only be waiting for me again in a land where there is no pain or death." Bert managed a faint smile and slipped into a peaceful slumber. Momentarily she rested her face beside his on the pillow, perhaps for the final time. She did not know.

It was Arthur who was with Bert at the last. He awoke and found comfort in Arthur's presence. There was a flicker of gladness in eyes where lips could no longer speak. For a moment that would last Arthur always the two young homesteaders looked at each other—and then Bert was gone. Arthur's faith was simple and seldom spoken. Somehow, though, he just knew that for his dear friend there was an outstretched hand on the other side. And that thought eased somewhat the terrible burden of loss.

There was no money for much of a funeral. Both Arthur and Bertha had spend all they had, so Bert was placed in a simple casket and buried in the small Clear Lake cemetery a few miles from their claims. Sympathy was genuine, for few at the graveside had not placed some loved one taken early in the earth.

Bertha spent the next few days with Amy, but then necessarily came the return to the cabin where Bert had brought her with such high expectations but a brief year before. She paused to look out over their acres and the rolling plains beyond. Commanding the landscape, there was the mount of denial, where their dreams had died in the freak roll of the wagon wheel. It was spring but the brightness of the day only mocked the gloom of her spirit. How did the sun dare to shine, as if her heart were not broken, her world come apart, with nothing but the loneliness of this homestead to greet her with each dawn!

But the relatives and neighbors were to make a big difference in the weeks and months ahead. Arthur and Luke helped with the plowing and planting, and a family named Cartwright took an especial interest in the young widow. William and Margaret Cartwright had come out in 1911 from Fort Scott, Kansas, along with son Willie, daughter Eva, and granddaughter Nina. They had a place nine miles or so north of Geraldine, near the Clear Lake community. Eva had buried a young husband back in Kansas and so knew the grief in Bertha's heart. The Cartwrights were there at Bert's committal services and insisted that they be of help. Nina was a lively thirteen and budding into young womanhood. She had dreams of other things than picking up rocks and doing household chores and so jumped at the suggestion that she live with Bertha for awhile.

Nina proved to be good medicine for Bertha's bruised spirit, with her incessant chatter about boys, the neighbors, church, school, parties, and whatever else enlivened her interests. Her infectious spirit stirred Bertha's own instinctive buoyant attitude toward life and often laughter returned to the little cabin Bert had built. Sometimes, at Nina's urging, they would go out and race their ponies with the wind, hair whipping around their faces, and hearts pulsating with the elemental joy of being alive. So a bond grew between the 26-year-old woman and the 13-year-old kid of exuberant energy. It was mostly in the quiet of the night, when her young companion was asleep, that the tears would come and Bertha would yearn for the strong arms she once had known. Even in her sleep grief shaped the dreams that eventually would yield to the healing grace of time.

Increasingly Bertha's days filled up with little Arthur's care and the work on the homestead. One day Nina talked Bertha into sprucing up the cabin and having a party. So they dug deep into trunks for a pretty dress and for whatever could be found to brighten the little drab room. They made cookies, popped corn, and prepared for the neighbors. Soon the cabin was crowded and groups gathered outside to talk and watch the children play. Some games required songs like "Skip to my Lou" and "Pig in the Parlor" and then the adults joined in. Such times of gathering healed the loneliness and softened the asperities of the hard life of the plains.

Arthur was glad for this time of relaxation. His days had been long and exhausting in trying to prove up on both homesteads. Most evenings he had little energy left, even to prepare a hot meal, but would eat whatever was available, and bone weary, collapse on his bed. One day Bertha and Nina decided to clean his cabin, wash and mend his clothes and have a hot meal waiting for him when he came home that evening. All had been accomplished by nightfall, but Arthur didn't show up. So they had their meal and decided to spend the night there.

Around midnight Bertha awoke with a start. It was no dream. She had heard a man scream just outside the cabin. Tense, trembling, she sat up in bed, in the process awakening Nina who wanted to know what had happened and why was she sitting up in bed. Before Bertha could answer, another blood-curdling cry pierced the cabin walls. Nina threw herself into Bertha's arms, crying, "Oh, there's a crazy man outside!" Bertha's heart pounded as she thought of their being all alone on the prairie with whatever was outside. There was no lock on the door which might be flung open at any moment. Then in the moonlight she saw little Arthur in his makeshift bed on the floor and fear was fused with motherly resolve. Whoever or whatever that was would get to him over her dead body.

"Get up, Nina, and follow me." In the semi-dark she felt near the stove and found a steel poker and then a butcher knife on the cupboard. Handing the poker to Nina, she whispered, "Come on. Whoever it is we're going to meet them outside."

Nervously they edged the door open and slipped through it. Crouching near the wall, the two women, hearts racing, inched noiselessly along the front side of the cabin, poker and knife clutched in readiness for action. Bertha peeked around the corner but no attacker was in sight. He had to be on the other side, so they crept along, terrified but determined to kill or be killed. At the next corner, Bertha gripped her knife harder and jumped around, but again no one was in sight, not even a suspicious shadow. She relaxed a little as Nina whispered, "Where is he?"

"I don't know. Let's go around the cabin again. Maybe he heard us coming." Still on their guard, they rounded the cabin once more and then searched over near the corral. Perhaps he was hiding underneath the wagon. But the mystery crazy man had vanished, so they returned to the cabin and to bed, laying their weapons within easy reach.

Neither got much sleep for the rest of the night and were glad to see morning come. About mid-morning Arthur rode in from an all-night search for a neighbor's horses that had strayed off to the mountains. He was surprised to see Bertha and Nina but even more taken back by their greeting. An obviously agitated sister demanded to know where he had been all night. "We've been scared out of our wits!"

"Why? What's the matter?" he asked as he glanced around the place. "Everything looks all right to me."

"Well, it sure wasn't last night," Nina exclaimed. "There was a crazy man around here, screaming his head off, and trying to get into the cabin, but I guess we scared him away."

Nina's outburst brought a hint of a smile and a knowing look to his weary countenance. "You didn't happen to see any birds flying around, did you?"

"Suppose we did," Bertha shot back, remembering having seen a bird or two around the cabin but failing to see any connection and certainly nothing humorous in the situation.

"That was your villain," Arthur assured her. "Every so often they come around here, mostly at night, and their scream is almost human. I got a real scare when I first heard them."

The two women accepted his explanation, though it took a bit of doing to acknowledge that their fearsome visitor of the night before was only a bird!

The crisis over, Bertha and Nina at least had the satisfaction of preparing a hot meal for Arthur and leaving him with a spruced-up cabin and supply of clean clothes.

The days remained full for both Arthur and Bertha during that summer of 1915. Luke helped whenever he could with the work on the two homesteads and Amy and Bertha visited often and compared notes on child raising. Bertha worked out whenever she could get a job house cleaning or caring for children. Some times she exchanged her labor for field help on her place.

One young homesteader who was especially interested in helping her was Nina's uncle, Willie Cartwright. In some respects, he was like Bert—open, jovial, musical, fun to be around. Willie worked as a matter of necessity and found no particular satisfaction in adding acres and accumulating property. A good place with sufficient livestock was nice to have but not fundamental to happiness. His idea of the good life involved plenty of time for visiting with neighbors and relatives. After a long day in the field, and a square meal, he enjoyed setting outside in the gathering twilight singing popular western songs. Since religion ran deep in his family, he also often tuned familiar hymns of Zion.

Bertha found comfort in her frequent visits to the Cartwright home, a kind of balm in Gilead for her troubled spirit. Willie's interest was obviously becoming romantic. He wanted Bertha in his arms and was sure that with his love, he could make her laugh again. Though she knew that she would probably remarry, it was too soon to think of anyone taking Bert's place. For the most part, Willie was understanding and prepared to wait.

Meanwhile, the wheat crops were beginning to look promising around Geraldine. With climbing prices the prospects were good. Then one day in mid-July dark thunderheads rolled in from the west. Lightning stabbed the earth, accompanied by driving rain and hail that soon destroyed an estimated half-million bushels in the county. Arthur, of course, was no stranger to such calamity. Often he had seen the violent moods of nature deal harshly with Ab's hopes for the harvest. One worked with what was left, trusting that warm weather would redeem soggy wheat from muddy soil and leave some kind of a crop.

As it happened, August did bring in a better crop than could have been expected. Since Arthur did not have a binder, he arranged to work for his neighbors, the McCardles, in exchange for their harvesting his wheat. Viola McCardle's father, commonly known as "Grandfather Lozier", and his two brothers had come out from Wisconsin in 1910 and taken up homesteads in the country east of Geraldine, then known as Winchell Springs. Arthur and Viola McCardle and family joined them two years later.

Stacking the wheat right was an important concern, to guard against spoilage until the threshing could be done. Since there was a scarcity of threshing rigs in the area, it might be winter before that could be accomplished. Now Grandfather Lozier was the acknowledged expert in this business and presided over many of the stacking operations. All day long he kept the other men busy feeding him the bundles of wheat which he placed in their appropriate places, tucking away and packing them down in the stack with his feet. Loose or broken bundles he placed in the center.

Disdaining a pitchfork, he went round and round on his hands and knees building up the stack to a diameter of 15 to 18 feet. If some unwary worker pitched him a bundle wrong end to or perchance hit him with it, the old man had some choice words for such inepitude. After the stack was finished, a long narrow stick was pushed down in the peak to hold the top on. All agreed that Grandfather Lozier's stacks were the work of an artist. More importantly, they kept the wheat dry under the most severe weather.

Threshing wheat was not without its hazards. There was the chance that a weak boiler on the steam thresher might blow or that a wayward spark might start a dreaded prairie fire. The previous year the Loziers and McCardles had engaged a man with a steam threshing rig. Just as he had finished their wheat and was leaving for another place, some sparks from the smoke stake ignited a blaze. A brisk wind out of the west whipped the flames through the neighboring grasslands. Within a half-hour the fire had spread a mile wide. Men with shovels, brooms, and sacks frantically fought the flames, which finally ran into plowed ground, and were brought under control.

It was hardly the fulfillment of his dreams but Arthur could view his first crop of Montana wheat with considerable satisfaction. To say the least, it was progress for homesteading on a shoestring. There was talk that prices would climb to two dollars a bushel and, if the war continued for long, perhaps even four dollars! So that one hundred dollar send-off by Ab might yet yield good dividends.

PROVING UP

That fall of 1915 Montana claimed another Henderson. Cecil, the third son and now twenty, was restless to be on his own. He had had enough of living at home and working around for neighboring farmers. In many respects, he was like Bertha, tall and slender, full of life and a good mixer, and rather too independent of spirit to put up with Ab's patriarchal ways. More often than not, father and son could not discuss a project without ending in a squabble. Cecil's sense of humor also ran to pranks which the elder Henderson did not always appreciate. Then there was younger brother Rolland with whom he had frequent spats.

It seemed like the right time to make his move. Ab's Louisiana experiment had not worked out as expected, so he had relocated again on a section of land near Thayer, Kansas. Cecil figured the folks could make do without him and decided to try Montana. The letters home were generally enthusiastic and Arthur had invited him to stay at his homestead until he was old enough to file on his own claim. Arthur had already eyed some adjoining land which he thought would be just right for his younger brother. The two had always gotten along well at home, so it seemed like a good arrangement.

Cecil arrived unannounced at the depot in Geraldine in mid-

September. He knew that Amy's place was nearer, about nine miles out of town, so he asked for directions and headed out across the prairie. The big sky was clear but a cold westerly wind quickened his pace. The young Kansan was glad for three homestead shacks along the way where he could get warm and verify his route. Doubts about his journey faded in the enthusiasm of Amy's welcome, though she did chide him for not letting her know when he was coming. Around the supper table and long into the evening, he shared news from home. The next morning Luke hitched up the team and he and Amy drove Cecil over to Arthur's place.

Soon the younger brother was acquainted with the spartan life of the Montana homestead. With the harvest in, there was the daily routine of clearing rocks, plowing more acres, getting in wood for the winter, and doing odd jobs for neighboring farmers and ranchers. Arthur still depended upon working out at $40 or so a month to keep something in the larder and to have money for seed in the spring. Much of what the brothers ate came out of cans, and it was usually at suppertime the younger Henderson with his robust appetite missed home most and questioned the great sacrifice involved in pioneering.

One morning, as fall sharpened the air, Cecil got a job more to his liking than wrestling rocks, more in keeping with his notions of a life in the West. Arthur was over at Highwood for a day or two and a neighbor needed some horses rounded up. Fences were still not that common in the country and stock ran loose on free range. Milk cows were driven home each evening and beef cattle usually stayed close, but horses might wander thirty or forty miles away in search of greener grazing. Riders kept an eye open for brands and could often save each other unnecessarily long hours in the saddle. Unfortunately, Cecil was unacquainted and had no such guidance as he searched an unfamiliar terrain.

What he thought would only take a few hours had led him far afield by dark, with only a thin blanket for protection and no provisions in his saddle bag. He had not even thought to bring a gun to kill a jackrabbit or to discourage a prowling predator from getting too close. Wolves were still around, though their numbers were rapidly thinning out along with the dwindling herds of antelope. Deer were about non-existent in the area. There was no open season on antelope between 1903 and 1934, though that did not keep the homesteader from savoring an antelope steak from time to time. Cecil would have gladly traded his birthright for one and some hot biscuits. As it was, cold and hunger prevented much sleep and at daybreak the disconsolate young Kansan continued his search. Those fool horses, he muttered, could be anywhere in these endless gullies. His stomach burned with neglect and he was about to turn back when, at least, he found his quarry. Late that evening he was back home, much the wiser for his experience, and eager to do justice to Arthur's hard biscuits and beans.

Cecil's ordeal caused his brother to remark on one of the big worries of homesteaders. Getting lost in a vast county without roads or fences was no small concern, especially during the winter months. Often an anxious homestead wife hung a lantern outside for her man returning home after dark. There were no weather forecasts, and Montana's capricious winters made travel hazardous. More than one farmer left for Benton or Geraldine to get a wagon load of supplies during a January thaw only to get caught in a savage storm before he could return. Then his family, huddled in a little shack, had an anxious vigil, sometimes for days, until he was able to get back.

A few days later Amy and Luke dropped by and Cecil, always ready with a story, told them of his adventure, concluding that the country needed more fences. Luke demurred, allowing that fences did not make good neighbors, and he had his own story to prove the point. A rancher decided to fence a road that saved Luke and neighboring farmers several miles in getting to Geraldine. When he heard about it, he decided to discuss the situation with a friend who, like him, stood about six feet and weighed in about 200 pounds. His burley neighbor was feeding the cows as he drove up.

"Good morning, Bill," I greeted him. "This looks like a good day to take our eggs to Geraldine. Care to drop that fork and come along?"

"Sure thing, Luke," he grins at me. "I could stand a day away from this grind. And I kinda like to see if our good friend down the road really did put up a fence."

"I sorta had that in mind, too," I nodded. "I'm kinda curious how serious he is about closing our road."

Bill collects some eggs and climbs in beside me. Sure enough down the forbidden road we come to a fence and gate guarded by this bold baron of Chouteau County. I hand Bill the reins and jump down.

"Bill and I thought we'd go to Geraldine on this road because it is closer."

The gatekeeper eyes us for a long moment and then swings the gate open. "You're right, fellas," he says, "I guess it is a little closer for you."

"Down the road Bill chuckles, "Do you think he'll be there when we come back?"

"I doubt it," I reply. "He knew why we came this way and probably decided that his damn fence wasn't such a good idea after all."

Cecil remained unconvinced about fences but was determined, if
humanly possible, to avoid another cold night under the stars.
Henceforth, he intended that his travels would keep him within
distance of a friendly cabin before nightfall. Boyish, restless, and
craving company, he stayed at home as little as possible when Arthur was gone, but made the rounds of relatives and neighbors.

Not long after his roundup adventure, he found himself at
Bertha's cabin just as an autumn sunset was fading in a profusion of
colors. Bertha was away working but Nina and mother Eva happened to be there. They had just finished the chores and were setting
down for supper. "That sure smells good," Cecil announced as he
poked his head in around the door.

"We hope it's good," Nina grinned. "Come in and we'll set a place
for you.

Cecil did not need a second invitation but quickly washed the
dust from his hands and face, brushed his hair, and was at the table.
"One thing I like about this country," he declared with notable enthusiasm, "No matter where you are at meal time you eat." Nina gig-
gled at an opportunity too good to miss. "And you're usually near
somebody's table, morning, noon, and night."

Cecil laughed and admitted that she had him sized up about right,
but Eva was quick to apologize. "Nina shouldn't have said that.
You're always welcome to eat with us and I know the other settlers
appreciate your cheerful, carefree spirit. You're good medicine for
the blues."

Nina and Cecil kept the table talk on the light side, with the news
of local happenings rather than of the price of wheat or of the Euro-
pean war. When at last he announced that it was time to be going,
Eva spoke up quickly. "We'd like to have you stay for the night.
Nina and I don't normally stay alone. There's probably nothing to
be afraid of, but we'd feel better with a man in the house."

Her invitation so surprised him that he fumbled for something to
say. Finally, he remembered seeing a pile of hay in the shed and
offered to bed down there.

"Oh! No!," Eva insisted. "You can sleep with us here in the cabin
where it is warm. We'll make a bed for you on the floor. That seemed to settle the matter and was definitely to Nina's liking. Not every
night did a girl have a young man so close to her bed, and she kept
up a constant chatter until Eva began to reconsider the wisdom of

her hospitality and threaten to banish Cecil to the shed. For the second time since his arrival in Montana, he spent a wakeful night in unusual surroundings. But he had to admit that it was better this time than lying cold all alone out under the stars.

Other visitors frequented Bertha's dwelling during the fall of 1915. Several suitors pursued the young widow with passion, but Willie Cartwright finally prevailed with his gentleness and understanding. Nobody could stir her womanhood like Bert, but she could feel safe and loved in Willie's arms. Homesteading was rough without a husband and she was tired of all the working around. Besides little Arthur needed a father. So they were married on November 2 in a simple ceremony with a few relatives looking on.

Willie's place was a big improvement on the little shack Bert had built. The house had two sizeable rooms and was lathed and plastered. A deep well close by was equipped with a gasoline pump and provided ample water. There were several milk cows, plus turkeys and chickens and a large vegetable garden. Willie and his father had adjoining places and had done considerable to improve their homesteads since filing on them in 1911. The older Cartwright even had a small lake on his property which was handy for watering the stock until it dried up in 1917.

Before settling down, Bertha wanted a sort of honeymoon back in Kansas. Home ties were still strong and it was time to see the family again and have them meet Willie. Train fare, she told him, was more important to her than a diamond ring. They found Ab and Mame in the midst of preparations for a public sale. With his family getting smaller, Ab was thinking of semi-retirement and wanting to get rid of an accumulation of farm machinery and excess livestock. He was planning on a place of only forty acres. Bertha and Willie enjoyed helping and stayed until a successful sale was over.

Around the dinner table and in the evening talk often turned to life in Montana. Ab had to be impressed with reports of 35 to 40 bushels of wheat per acre. Claude, next to Arthur in age, was especially interested since he was now married and wife Clara wanted to put some distance between them and the in-laws. For Rolland, now 17, the mountains sounded like a welcome change from Kansas, while the four younger children listened to their older sister and new brother-in-law and conjured up their own pictures of a far-off, fabled cowboy land. Too soon the visit was over and with winter threatening the newlyweds headed back home for their homestead. From time to time some bit of scenery would bring back sad memories of her first trip to Montana and the pain of loss. Then

Bertha would reach out a hand to Willie and, in the reassurance of the arm he placed around her, she would feel good about their life together.

The winter of 1915-16 brought a lot of snow and cold to the Geraldine country and accentuated the discomforts of life in a homestead shack. The weather found cracks Arthur thought he had filled, and many mornings he and Cecil awoke to newly sifted snow on the cabin floor. The younger Henderson was content to linger in the warmth of the blankets and to trust to Arthur's ambition to be up and doing—especially to break the ice in the water bucket and get a hot fire going. Sometimes, though, it didn't work when Arthur figured it was about Cecil's turn and, with a foot in the back propelled him onto the cold floor. He would laugh as his younger brother danced around trying to keep warm while getting a fire started.

Cecil just couldn't figure why his brother always had to be doing something. The obvious place to be on a cold morning was in bed. Even in good weather, a fellow needed some time to wake up and think about the day's activities. But Arthur had this queer notion that daylight meant work, and he seemed to have a genius for finding jobs for both of them. When all else failed, there was wood to be cut and those damned rocks to be wrestled off the land. Winter slowed him down some, but not enough to Cecil's liking.

There were, of course, the fun times when the two brothers would saddle up and get better acquainted with the surrounding countryside. Now and then Arthur would point to an odd shaped rock bearing the letter "R" and observe that it was a trail marker to guide the cavalry between forts in the early days. As a matter of fact, an old military trail ran across a corner of Arthur's place. Cecil liked hunting with his brother and especially enjoyed the fishing trips over on Arrow Creek which could last long into the evening. If they were lucky, they might glimpse a herd of wild horses that still roamed the area with a big black stallion in command. Stationed on a hill to detect intruders, he could have his band rounded up and soon out of sight. There was a fascination in the grace and freedom of effortless motion that made Cecil with his own fleetness of foot want to race with them. There was also, as the brothers watched, a tinge of sadness at this vanishing part of the West.

Twice a month or so Arthur and Cecil took a trip to Geraldine which also helped break the monotony of homestead life. It was only 18 miles into town, but it meant the better part of a day. Geraldine in 1915 was bustling with activity. Settled just two years before, it could already boast a population nearing 400 and a prosperous business district. Centered in rolling prairie country, equidistant from Lewistown and Great Falls and 28 miles from Fort Benton, it showed every indication of not being just another homestead town. As the *Lewistown Daily News* observed, "Geraldine...is a live one, having city parks and a spendid up-to-date appearance, growing rapidly."

Even its name was auspicious, honoring Mrs. William G. Rockefeller, whose husband held a large interest in the Milwaukee railroad which gave Geraldine its first boost. The line built a depot there and people wagoned in from all around to celebrate its dedication on New Year's Eve of 1913. There was nothing that excited and gladdened the people of the area more than the coming of the railroad. It was the surest harbinger of a prosperous future. Before the year was out, wheat was moving by rail out of Geraldine, sparing area farmers the long haul to Benton.

Not surprisingly, one of the initial business ventures had been a saloon, whose proprietor spent his first night in town sleeping on top of his wagon load of beer, hopefully to discourage pilferers. Opened in a tent, the saloon soon occupied more permanent quarters. In 1915, in a spectacular burst of activitity, Geraldine had a total of some 85 commercial and professional ventures and was doing an annual business of more than one million dollars. Strung along Main Street were three general stores, a bank, six restaurants, two hotels, a hardware and furniture store, drug store, jeweler, and offices for two doctors, one dentist, one lawyer, and five insurance agents. Elsewhere one could find blacksmiths, plumbers, electricians, pool halls, lumber yards, livery stables, grain elevators, and so on. *The Geraldine Review*, begun in 1913, provided a weekly report of happenings in the area.

Where once cattle and sheep grazed on nutritious grassland or travelers stopped to quench their thirst at the nearby springs, gas lights on iron posts now lined graded streets with cement sidewalks. Prominent among the buildings along Main Street was Farmers State Bank, opened early in a small wooden structure but now possessing a handsome brick edifice. The bankers there and elsewhere in homestead land were enthused by the good times and ready to loan money on wheat crops for added acreage or to buy farm implements. Soon Uncle Sam would be calling for an all-out effort to feed the Allies and that would mean more machinery to increase the harvests. Later when Montana boys would be called up in record numbers and labor would be scarce, more machinery on easy credit would be essential to handle larger crops.

Arthur looked with longing at the gleaming new plows in the mercantile store but knew that he had to make do with Buster and his old one. It was not his disposition to go heavily into debt but to make improvements when he had the means to do so. Cecil usually planned on a stop at one of the restaurants where for thirty cents he could have a change from Arthur's limited fare. A visit at the barber shop meant another twenty-five cents. On those rare occasions when he felt flush, he could get a pair of pants for seventy cents or shoes for one dollars and fifty cents. The post office had been in business for a year or two and sometimes yielded a letter from Kansas. Then, of course, there were supplies to be purchased. On one trip home from Geraldine, Cecil's horse spooked and bucked and before he got her quieted down, two weeks of groceries were scattered on the prairie.

Other aspects of community life were not of particular concern to the young homesteaders. Geraldine now had a local government and mayor. The Northern Montana Telephone Company was stringing some lines in town. The Methodists had organized a congregation and were holding services for a while in the depot. The Roman Catholics had a church under way and there was a rapidly growing public school. Of great interest to Cecil were the social events he heard about or read about in an old copy of *The Geraldine Review* —the parties and holiday celebrations or the traveling vaudeville and ministrel shows. It was at such times that the 18 miles out on the prairie seemed a high price to pay for the homestead way of life.

There were, of course, the Saturday night barn dances attended by all ages. Sometimes Cecil succeeded in getting Arthur to go along. A drink or two and a girl to waltz around did a lot for Cecil's morale, except on one occasion where he got into a fight over his dancing partner and had to nurse a sore jaw for several days. Many homesteaders and especially the women came from temperance or prohibition backgrounds and contributed to the process of Montana going dry by 1918. Some others, though, demonstrated both defiance and ingenuity in concocting their home brews or getting booze from over the Canadian border after the enactment of the Eighteenth Amendment. More than one farm boy would later remember the barrels of "mash" carefully concealed in manure piles aging in preparation for the still, as they would also recall the strict warnings not to sample the illicit stuff. At night the enterprising moonshiner watched the highway for blinking headlights as the signal that a delivery was to be made. At times he would disappear for days or weeks on end when it was rumored that the federal boys were around.

Early spring found Amy and Luke making a trip back to Kansas before planting time. Mame had not seen her namesake granddaughter and had been urging that it was about time. Needless to say, she was the center of attention. Amy appreciated the milder Kansas weather and confided to Ab and Mame that sooner or later her health would necessitate a move back. It was a thoroughly enjoyable visit, but after two weeks Luke began to fidget in a way that Ab could understand. There was much that needed to be done before the spring planting and he was worried, too, about his livestock. It looked like it could be another good year in Montana, perhaps with record crops and prices. As it turned out, it was the last good year for many homesteaders.

1916 also brought Cecil's twenty-first birthday and the long-awaited opportunity to file on his own claim. Arthur had managed to keep available some acreage adjoining his land and the Arthur McCardles. There was a small lake on the place as testimony to the wet years. A lake or watering hole was a big plus for the homesteader who looked forward to a herd of horses and cows to go along with his wheat acreage. Soon Cecil had his own shack, built with the assistance of Luke's father who was visiting from Kansas. Arthur helped him dig a well which yielded brackish water. Then the two brothers turned their attention to breaking up some sod. By now Arthur had acquired several horses and a sixteen-inch riding plow. They could average four or five acres a day and before long had twenty acres ready for planting. Cecil surveyed their accomplishment and took pride in the thought that he was now in the homesteading business on his own.

The prospects were both exciting and sobering. Looking out over the land that would become his when he had made the final proof, he could appreciate for the first time what Ab had often told his boys about "root, hog, or die." It would be a long haul starting from scratch, but Arthur was doing it. He would have to continue to work around for living money, but he had relatives to help him prove up on the place.

He also had good neighbors in the McCardles. They had been on their homestead since 1912 and were about as prairie-wise as anyone around. They, too, had begun with next to nothing. Arthur McCardle arrived with enough money in his pocket to put a wood floor in their sod house and that was about all. Fortunately, Viola's relatives, the Loziers, lived nearby and loaned them horses and plows to put in crops. They did have the best well for three miles or so around which they shared with Arthur and Cecil and other neighbors. They had run the gamut of homestead hardships and troubles. Their first winter brought blizzards and prolonged cold. Their wood supply dwindled and then was gone. They survived by burning old cottonwood fence posts from an abandoned pasture.

When it rained hard, rivulets ran down the walls of their sod shack and pots and pans around the room caught muddy water seeping through above. The constant plop-plop of water got on one's nerves, especially if there was worry that continued rain might bring down the whole roof. They also had their hassles with Russian thistles and prairie dogs and prairie fires. Unwelcome visitors posed another kind of problem. One day Viola had to get the attention of a drunken cowboy with her 30-30 rifle, and she kept a revolver concealed in her apron whenever a certain sheepherder who persisted in running his flocks on their place came around. She had learned to be very proficient in its use.

An occasional small hunting party of Indians with camping gear piled high in their wagons crossed the McCardle and Henderson places but caused little concern. Quite a different matter was the appearance of gypsies with their wagons which caused mothers to chase their children inside. For some reason, the fear persisted all around the country that gypsies would kidnap the young.

Tragedy had struck the McCardles and Loziers in early 1915 when Viola's brother, Pete Lozier, rolled his new Model T touring car and he and his son were killed. Husband Arthur was in the vehicle but escaped without serious injury. That fall another accident involving the same ill-fated Model T put the McCardles' son, Leon, in the Benton hospital for three months. Such adversities were made a bit more bearable by the kind of neighboring that went on. The cold January night when Pete Lozier was killed an area farmer walked or rode several miles to bring Viola the sad news and to stay with her until he felt she would be all right. So the McCardles, seasoned by hardship, could appreciate the uphill struggle of their two young neighbors from Kansas.

That same spring of 1916 Arthur found himself involved in an effort to build a school for the area children. His own education had been cut short at the eighth grade, which was common with farm boys whose help was needed home. Bachelor though he was, he shared the concern that something must be done. A meeting was called at his place of all families with children of school age to discuss plans for a building. It was decided that if the county would furnish the materials, the people assembled would provide the labor. The county fathers agreed and soon the Sunnyside School was a reality. It sat near Arrow Creek breaks for ten years until, hitched to 24 horses, it was dragged across the prairie to a new location.

No less than ten different teachers, all women but one, served the little one-room school during the years it was at Arrow Creek. Homestead wives with teaching experience often took the opportunity to augment family income during the "proving up" time. Other adventurous young school "marms" came to Montana from the East. Whether locally or from afar, the teacher had to be about the most resourceful person around. For fifty or sixty dollars a month, she was educator, disciplinarian, janitor, repairman, nurse, and handler of any and all emergencies. The state prescribed a rigid curriculum which had to be taught without benefit of adequate instructional equipment and supplies. Eighth graders would be expected to pass an exam before moving on to boarding school and further education in town.

In addition, the teacher faced a formidable task in socializing some of her charges. Children came from homestead shacks where when a stranger knocked there would be a scurrying for the protection of the pantry or a place underneath the table. There were many rough edges to be smoothed. Twice a year, the county superintendent would come around to check on conditions and, perhaps, give a boost to morale. Later, the visits of the county health nurse found reluctant children lining up for inspections of mouth, nose, and ears, fearful she might also want to look at their toes.

Sunnyside was above average for homestead schoolhouses, with shed on back and, of course, with the ubiquitious outhouse standing guard in a corner and breaking the barreness of the schoolyard. During the warm months children frequented it to the limits of the teacher's patience but avoided it as long as possible when the weather turned bad. Sometimes, though, privies for boys and girls were located in opposite ends of a horse barn and that made for greater protection. A fence usually rimmed the school yard, which might also contain a swing or a giant stride. If the district was prosperous, a "teacherage" of two rooms or so might adjoin the school and spare the teacher the need for boarding around.

Little schoolhouses like Sunnyside not only symbolized culture on the homestead frontier, but they were also the focus of community life. There farmers and their families rode in for meetings, Christmas programs, parties, dances, box socials, and an occasional preacher or Sunday School worker. In the newly built structure Arthur and his neighbors gathered to discuss mail service from Geraldine to their area. It left much to be desired since letters from town traveled a roundabout route of 140 miles via Great Falls and Fort Benton before reaching their destination. A more direct route as the crow flies seemed the better part of common sense. Sufficient petitioners were found to gain approval for such a rural route which opened in September.

1916 continued the pattern of ample rainfall. Since 1909, precipitation averaged about 16 inches a year. Wheat was coming in at 25 bushels and better an acre, and 1915 had seen a record harvest of over 42 million bushels. Prices were climbing to $2.00 a bushel and the future looked rosy indeed. In the fall, long lines of homesteader wagons waited to unload. Prosperity in the county was evidenced by bank deposits which amounted to better than $1600 for every man, woman, and child in Fort Benton, the highest such per capita in the nation!

Arthur had been on his homestead nearly three years and, like his neighbors, regarded the future with optimism. Unlike many who came without a farming background, he knew that nature could be cruel and capricious; yet the contagion of good times was everywhere and gave little encouragement to caution or doubt. But Arthur had other things on his mind besides wheat as fall lengthened into winter and another year rolled around. He had been riding over to the Delaska Cottrell place to visit with son Murry, but soon found his interest shifting to younger sister Lulu. Brown-eyed and lively, she was the oldest daughter and fourth child in a family of seven.

The Cottrells came originally from Oklahoma but had relocated in Iowa before moving to Montana. Oldest son Glenn came first in 1914 and worked on ranches in the Square Butte area. Delaska Cottrell and Murry arrived a year later, in August, by immigrant car at Square Butte. In addition to household goods, farm machinery, and various livestock, he brought his prized Morgan driving team, "Spanish" and "Maude". The latter was the family favorite as she was an excellent saddle horse. Roba Cottrell and the remaining five children came the following month. The family settled on an established farm in the Hawarden district east of Geraldine.

Arthur was now 25 and somewhat settled into the ways of bachelorhood. Quiet and sober on the whole, his life had been rather predictable to date. But this spirited teenager with the engaging smile and popular ways with her peers could make a difference in his plans. At least, it wasn't too long before he had gotten up courage to ask her for a ride. She astride Maude and he on faithful Buster rode out on the first of many rides.

Cecil's first—and, as it proved, last—year on the homestead left him with enduring memories of pioneer life. That summer of 1916 he worked for considerable periods on ranches in the region. One time he returned home to find that the neighbors had let a school teacher move into his shack. Gallantly, he let her stay and moved on to the next job. That winter, another visitor was blown in by a blizzard and stayed with Cecil the better part of a week. Then a neighbor had to rush his pregnant wife to the hospital in Benton where she died in childbirth. Cecil labored to have a grave ready for the bodies of mother and child which were thoroughly frozen by the time they were back home.

By the spring of 1917 he was having second thoughts about homesteading. He remained restless and was not willing to make Arthur's kind of commitment to the land. Tragedy and hardship rested heavily upon his still boyish spirit. Brother Claude had been writing from Kansas of his desire to relocate, so Cecil invited him to come on and take over his place. He would turn in his claim and Claude could file on it. When Claude and his family arrived, Cecil got a job on the Great Northern and worked for the railroad until his call into the service. Claude was more like Arthur, stable and settled, and he would remain on the homestead for the next five years or so, before returning to Kansas. Meanwhile, the spring of 1917 would bring great changes in the lives of many Montana homesteaders.

THE WAR YEARS

Four months after Arthur's arrival in Montana, an assassin's bullet triggered the gigantic struggle which his generation would remember as the Great War. Few on the homestead frontier or, for that matter, in the country at large, realized what was happening, that one age was dying in the thunder of battle and another was struggling in uncertain birth. For those like young Herbert Hoover living in England who viewed the past 25 years in western Europe as among the happiest in history, the coming of the war was a real shaking of the foundations. Actually, the imperialistic rivalries of the great powers had been making of Europe a veritable tinder box inviting ignition. While some statesmen trusted to the existing alliances to forestall war, other observers believed it was just a question of time. The slaying of the heir to Austria-Hungary's throne on June 28, 1914, by a young Serbian terrorist provided the spark and brought the conflagration. Russia, France, and Great Britain were soon arrayed against the Central Powers, mainly, Germany and Austria-Hungary. President Wilson promptly invoked neutrality and called upon shocked and dismayed Americans to be impartial in thought and deed.

Most Americans believed that it was not their struggle and were thankful for the vast ocean separating them from old world disasters. Generally, cultural and economic ties bound the country more closely to Great Britain, while many Americans remembered the aid France had given to the cause of independence. The name of Layafette still stirred their emotions. German militarism, symbolized by the spike-helmeted, mustached Kaiser Wilhelm II, had been getting unfavorable press in the United States for its arms buildup and its confrontations with American interests in the Far East and elsewhere. Yet, for the eleven million of German and Austrian descent, there was bound to be sentimental ties to the Fatherland. Many had settled in the West, including the thousands living on the farmlands of Montana. There were also the Irish-Americans, numbering over four million, with a sizeable community in Butte and in western Montana, who were strongly opposed to anything British. Support for the Allies was strengthened by the German assault on unoffending Belgium, and later, in May, 1915, the sinking of the British liner *Lusitania* with 128 Americans on board. From the beginning of hostilities, Allied war propaganda had better access to public opinion in the United States and lost no opportunity to build up and, on occasion, fictionalize Hun atrocities.

Few Americans remained impartial in thought and deed, and, furthermore, it proved to be most difficult for the government to maintain a neutral stance. For a depression-wary country, war meant the opportunity for a new prosperity, but soon American trade was caught between Allied blockades and German submarine zones. Britain proceeded to redefine blockade and contraband of war to suit her own interests and began seizing American ships headed for the continent. While the Wilson administration was rankled by this disregard for neutral rights, powerful pressures moved it closer to the Allied side. There were the underlying pro-British sympathies, but basically it was a matter of economics. The trade with the Allies was expanding enormously, while that with the Central Powers was dwindling into insignificance. Even with the British harassments, there was a handsome profit to be made. Business men were soon clamoring to advance loans for Allied purchase of American goods, including Montana wheat. At first reluctant, Wilson then agreed. Later he would point out the loss of cargoes to the British might threaten profits which, after all, was only property, while the German submarines were taking lives. That, in the long run, brought America into the war.

For Arthur and his neighbors, the coming of the war for the most part meant an unprecedented prosperity, with the price of wheat moving above $2.00 a bushel. Later, food administrator Herbert

Hoover would establish a base price of $2.20. That coupled with the soaring demand brought the plowing up of many additional acres. Elsewhere in Montana, the mining towns and lumber camps were also hitting a record production. Such good times would not come again until Hitler's legions renewed the attack upon the West.

Wilson barely won re-election in 1916 with his party sounding a campaign slogan that he had kept the country out of war. Thereafter, he sought through mediation to bring the adversaries to the conference table. In stirring speeches, he urged "peace without victory" as the only course of action that would not lead to future wars of retaliation. All nations must be treated as equals and all peoples must be given the precious right of self-determination of government. Both sides, however, had invested too much to compromise victory, to come away from the battlefield without the spoils of war. Germany had not succeeded in a quick victory and was being hurt by the blockade and so announced the resumption of submarine warfare against *all* ships in declared danger zones. When four unarmed American merchantmen were sunk in March of 1917, Wilson wearily called the 65th Congress into special session on April 2. The war resolution passed both houses with large majorities, with Montana's Jeannette Rankin casting one of the fifty negative votes in the House. Her action was consistent with a lifelong commitment to pacifism. "I want to stand by my country," she declared, "but I cannot vote for war." She was booed that day and booed again when she cast the *only* vote against war in 1941!

Wilson had worked hard for peace, but when hostilities came he proved to be an able and inspiring wartime leader. He was at his eloquent best as the moral idealist trumpeting the great crusade to win "the war to end all wars," "to make the world safe for democracy," and then articulating his fourteen points and more for the shaping of the post-war world. Meanwhile, his administration provided vigorous leadership in the mobilization of manpower and resources. Germany was counting upon delivering a knock-out blow before an unprepared United States could get geared up for battle. That proved to be a fatal assumption.

Montana stood high among the states in her response to the war. In proportion to population, she lead all others in the number of volunteers, while confused statistics caused the Selective Service to draft nearly twice the number due. Nearly 40,000 men went to war and with little disturbance, except for an anti-draft parade in Butte. More than 6000 came from the homesteads and most were unmarried men like Arthur. In proportion to population, Montana also lead all other states in lives lost. On the home front, Montanans responded generously to the several Liberty Bond drives, topping their quotas, and in the process stirred a frenzy of patriotism that sacrificed at times civil liberties. Few, if any, states paralleled the wartime hysteria which gripped parts of Montana.

The day after war was declared, Montana's national guard replacement was sworn into federal service as the 163rd Infantry Regiment, 41st Division. The unit had seen service recently on the Mexican border where Pancho Villa and his followers were causing tensions between the two countries. The regiment was assigned to protect transportation in the state, and then in the fall different battalions were sent to encampments back East preparatory to the 41st Division being shipped overseas. The men from Montana aboard the *USS Leviathan* [formerly the crack German liner *Vaterland)* landed at Liverpool in time for Christmas and then made it to France by year's end. There the regiment and the 41st were broken up in accordance with Allied strategy to use the Americans as replacements in the various combat divisions.

Wilson shared with many leaders a distaste for military conscription, but obviously there was no other way to put millions of soldiers on Europe's battlefields under the duress of time. After six weeks of hot debate, Congress enacted selective service and months later, in September, the first draftees reached training camps. That month the first Montana inductees went out to Camp Lewis near Tacoma, Washington, to join lumberjacks, homesteaders, cowboys, miners, and others from elsewhere in the Northwest. Camp Lewis was a sprawling affair built in ninety days despite the obstructionist tactics of the International Workers of the World. Big Bill Haywood's "Wobblies," as they were called, did not want a piece of the capitalists' war. The Camp had accommodations for 50,000 men in some 1750 buildings. In the early days there were not enough uniforms to go around and many draftees began their training in civilian clothes. It was here that Arthur would begin his military life in January of 1918, and Cecil somewhat later.

Meanwhile, the summer and fall of 1917 saw a markedly changing mood in Montana. Indicative of what was happening was a big Patriotic Day and Loyalty Parade in Lewistown on April 22. Tom Stout, editor of the local *Democrat News,* sounded the clarion call. "We are done with the days of a divided allegiance in this broad land of liberty. With our sacred honor and our liberties at stake, there can be but two classes of American citizens, patriots and traitors! Choose you the banner beneath which you will stand in this hour of trial." Unfortunately, with such sweeping distinctions, the mantle of disloyalty fell too easily on the innocent and guilty alike. There was no middle ground for the guardians of the republic as they prepared to do battle with foes real and imagined. Before the fears and hysteria they helped to foster had run their course, there would be a substantial erosion of liberty in the land of the brave and the home of the free.

That summer of 1917, over in Big Horn County, the minister of a newly organized German background church chanced to mention to a fellow preacher that he thought the war was wrong. That evening the church was padlocked and that night the minister and his family hid beneath a haystack. The next morning a friend spirited them away to Crow Agency and to a train bound for Portland, Oregon. Long afterward, the minister's widow vividly remembered the horror of the experience. The following preacher fared no better and was forced to leave town when the church was again locked up.

It was forbidden anywhere to worship in German and to teach German in the high schools. To make sure that this didn't happen, an unruly mob in Lewistown surrounded the Fergus County Free High School and confiscated and burned all German text books. Immigrants and suspect native-borns were obliged to prove their loyalty by the purchase of Liberty Bonds, flying the flag on their tractors, and, on occasion, kissing the flag in public. They were careful not to gather in any numbers in public since that might be construed as conspiracy in behalf of the Kaiser. Neighbors were encouraged to spy upon neighbors and report anything suspicious to the local loyalty or liberty committee. Recent immigrants who spoke little or no English had to be careful where they used their native tongue.

The concern for unAmerican activities also encompassed radical organizations like the I.W.W. and the Nonpartisan League. The "Wobblies" also known as the "I won't workers," were seen as menacing the war effort with strikes and other kinds of labor subversion. Many farmers viewed them as trouble makers and not to be trusted with a harvest. It was too easy to start a fire with a threshing machine. The feeling in Butte against them was especially acute and one evening an I.W.W. agitator was dragged from his bed and hung by a railroad trestle. Not only were his murderers never apprehended, but the lynching was noted in some area papers with evident approval.

The Nonpartisan League came out of Minnesota and the Dakotas preaching socialism to farmers who were now beginning to feel the effects of the encroaching drought. Crops were down in the fall of

1917, presaging what was to come, and many hard-hit homesteaders were willing to find the $16 dues to join the new organization. The League was active in Fergus County and had also picked up some converts in neighboring Chouteau County. Arthur was not among them, never being much of a joiner.

Prominent newspapers in the state contributed to the wartime emotionalism and even fantasy. Will Campbell of the *Helena Independent* perhaps went further than most in speculating when German airplanes hiding in the vastness of the surrounding mountains would zoom in and bomb the capitol. Tom Stout, who had made a trip with some congressmen to Belgium and France, lectured his readers repeatedly on the insidious ways of the German propaganda effort. On the political front, Montana had its state and county councils of defense and loyalty committees to encourage full cooperation with the war effort and to root out all disloyalty. In addition, in the early spring of 1918, in special session, the legislature passed a sedition law and a criminal syndicalism law, providing prison sentences for criticism of the war and the draft. Three months later, on May 16, 1918, and perhaps influenced by the Montana legislation, the Congress enacted a federal sedition law. Three years later, and with the heat of battle past, an embarrassed Congress would repeal this most restrictive law.

The Hendersons were safely English in their ancestry, so Arthur escaped any cloud of suspicion. For the most part, he was preoccupied with making a living and getting as good a crop as possible in the face of diminishing rainfall. Like all Montanans and people everywhere, he was learning to adjust to the new order of rationing on the home front, using less sugar, substituting rice flour for the real thing, and in general "Hooverizing" wherever possible. The name of the popular and efficient food administration had become synonymous with an all-out cooperation with the war effort.

Arthur intended after the harvest was in that fall to go to Fort Benton and sign up for the army. He felt strongly the call to duty, but it was also good to know that the government would give two months homesteading credit for every month of military service. Claude was now on Cecil's place and with his married status would undoubtedly stay put. He could keep an eye on his brother's homestead and scanty livestock while he was away. In this Arthur was more fortunate than many young bachelor homesteaders who had to turn their livestock loose to roam on public land. Most were branded, but the horses in particular ran with the wild herds and became a problem for the state.

On January 2, 1918, Arthur rode to Fort Benton and enlisted. His first days at Camp Lewis were complicated by the lack of a uniform and the theft of his suitcase which left him drilling in his best suit! As a member of Company D, 361st Infantry, 91st "Wild West" Division, he got his introduction to military life. He arrived in better physical condition than many recruits. He carried a muscular 140 pounds on a five-foot six-inch frame and had the stamina of years of hard work on the farm. The tutelage of the soil bred an endurance to see the task done. Long marches with a full pack over rugged terrain were no particular problem for him. It did take some training to become proficient in the use of firearms and, especially, to adjust to the gas mask. The ugly contraption, however, could be the difference in survival, so he made sure how to fasten it in place in a matter of seconds. Arthur had done enough hunting to possess considerably better marksmanship than the average recruit whom, the famous Alvin York once observed, could usually manage to miss everything but the sky!

For the first time in his life, Arthur was thrown in with a lot of people and, for the most part, he found it to be an exhilerating experience. The rich mix of personalities and backgrounds made for memories that would last a lifetime. "Henny," as his buddies soon called him, long afterward could remember the names of all the men in his company. One particularly unlikely association for the young homesteader was with a professional gambler who had been picked up in the draft. He saw no reason why that should interfere with his career and continued to ply his skills. He had an expensive gold watch which he used as a cushion against a run of bad luck. When he was losing, he would borrow money from Arthur and leave his watch for security. In a few days, good fortune would permit him to retrieve his property. Others in the company came from sheltered family life and suffered with the adjustment to army routine. Still others were a bit too rough-grained for Arthur's temperament to invite close association.

By June of 1918 the 91st was deemed battle-ready for the trenches 7000 miles away. At embarkation points on the east coast the men were given medical examinations and issued new equipment. They then were shipped to Liverpool and, following a brief stay at British rest camps, crossed the Channel in mid-July. The last leg of the journey was in crowded French 40 and 8 boxcars to camps where they received several weeks of intensive training in weaponry and use of gas masks before going to the front.

They arrived about the time the furious German offensive had spent its force. In May, Gen. Erick Ludendorff's drive had reached to within forty miles of Paris and threatened to knock France out of the war. American forces had arrived none too soon to help turn the tide at Chateau Thierry. Then in June came the heroics of the U.S. Marines at Belleau Wood and soon Marshall Foch was counter-attacking in the Second Battle of the Marne. With American divisions now poring into France, that was the beginning of the end for the Germans, though enormously bloody battles laid ahead.

In September, the "Wild West" 91st joined eight other American divisions now pouring into France, that was the beginning of the end for the Germans, though enormously bloody battles lay ahead. and brought him his only injury of the war. As he was charging an enemy position, he felt a sting on one hand and looked down to see blood flowing at the end of one finger dangling by a small piece of skin. In the protection of a trench, a buddy observed his predicament and offered help. "I got a little chewing tobacco in my pocket. Let's stick that thing back on and wrap it up in some tobacco." They completed the procedure with some gauze from the first aid kit and, days later, to Arthur's amazement, the finger was still fairly straight and somehow seemed to be healing all right.

Another near brush with disaster came when a bullet dented his helmet and knocked him unconscious. When he came to, lying in the mud and stench of the trench, his first impulse was to laugh as he fingered the dent and considered how closely death had passed him by. Still another time he nearly lost his pants when a bullet almost tore his cartridge belt away, destroying two shells in the process. War was often a matter of inches and Arthur lucked out.

The Yanks were at full strength with 1,200,000 soldiers for the final massive Meuse-Argonne offensive from late September to November 11. The fighting was espcially costly in the rugged Argonne Forest and the killed and wounded overall reached 120,000. Arthur tried to get used to the death around him, the stench of decaying flesh, the missing limbs, and the vacant eyes. The thought of killing another human being haunted him, especially if it were in a face to face encounter. Then one day he and a buddy lay outside their trench waiting for orders to move out when two Germans appeared less than a quarter of a mile away. Arthur's rifle was still damaged from a recent battle and not reliable. As they watched the enemy, Arthur whispered, "Shoot them before they get away." The soldier raised his rifle, aimed and waited. "Shoot!" Arthur urged again. "They won't be within range very long." The rifle wavered, was lowered, and then thrust at Arthur. "Here, you do it. I can't. I just can't do it." Arthur paused momentarily to reassure himself that this was war and a grim business of killing or being killed. Then he sighted in on the first German. Down he went and then the other. None of his buddies, he told himself, would die at their hands. He could not allow himself to think more than that.

There was another time when he came unexpectedly upon four of the enemy and was able to take them as prisoners of war. Deep down he felt better about that. He was glad for all the drilling he had received in the use of the gas mask, for one morning, just as they were stirring in their trench a bomb exploded nearby. He grabbed for his mask and had it quickly in place, but not before getting a few fumes. Others in the trench had inhaled more and had to be carried back for medical attention. Arthur found himself getting dizzy, weak, and nauseated, but was determined to stay at his post. Toward evening he had a high fever and sharp stomach pains. Then suddenly, it seemed that his muscles contracted and everything inside came up—undigested food and poison gas—awful to behold but it brought relief.

Arthur did not know it, but Cecil was also in the trenches during the Argonne offensive. He had been drafted some time after his brother enlisted but spent a short time at Camp Lewis. His division, the 77th, was from New York with Montana replacements, and was in France by late July, ill-prepared but badly needed to drive the Germans back. Cecil was still more boy than man, like many who marched beside him and cringed in fear on the eve of their first battle. His thoughts ran amuck but kept coming back to the home where Ab and Mame and the younger children would be sleeping in warm beds. No—Mame would be kneeling at her bedside, praying for the safety of her boys overseas. His own lips moved as he breathed a petition to the God of his childhood. Somehow that helped and he slept while others stirred in fretfulness around him.

When the charge came, Cecil found himself caught up in utter din and confusion, rising, lunging, falling, firing, stumbling over the dead and wounded. Bullets whined over his head—then suddenly they were over a small ridge and staring at a shattered hole on the other side. American artillery had found its mark and another German machine gun emplacement had been stilled. Cecil stared at death in all its grimness and horror. The mangled men did not look vicious. They were just like him, some hardly out of their teens, only in different uniforms. He felt sick and sad, but there was no time to agonize over the war. His buddies were charging past him and he must run, too.

Cecil's speed afoot was often utilized in carrying messages from one officer to another in the division. One night he and another messenger were caught in a search light. Instantly they froze and, then, as the light moved they hit the ground, just as a burst of bullets whined above them. Another time in early October, as he and his buddies were bedding down for another cold, wet night in the Argonne Forest, an exhausted soldier stumbled in, mumbling between labored breaths, that his battalion was surrounded by Germans. Taken to the captain, he related the plight of the famous "Lost Battalion." Several units of Cecil's New York 77th Division under the command of Major Charles W. Whittlesey, numbering about 600 men, had been attacking when they were cut off by the enemy. They had been holding out for several days, but were now without food and water and the ammunition was exhausted. They were under heavy fire but had refused German demands for surrender. A relief force was dispatched and rescued the battalion after its heroic five day stand and with a loss of 400 men.

Several days later Cecil's outfit was to be involved in the taking of a German-held town. The night before he found sleep difficult as he knew that tomorrow would bring some of the hardest fighting he had seen. So far he had been lucky, more than many of his buddies, but tomorrow could be different. Suddenly, a loud boom shook the earth around. Fire, heat, and light pierced the darkness, followed by the smell of gas. Cecil was knocked unconscious but a soldier beside him grabbed for his mask and put it in place. When he woke up again, he was in a hospital where he had been for several days. It was a close call, and by the time he was up again and feeling normal, the war was over.

Before the guns fell silent, a foe as unrelenting as the Germans was crowding the hospitals with American soldiers and sending many to early graves. Spanish influenza, as it was called, seemingly came out of nowhere, hitting the western front in the summer of 1918, and then getting worse as fall came. Before it had run its course, over 800,000 troops had been hospitalized, of whom 50,000 died of its complications, mainly pneumonia. That was more than were killed in battle (49,000). The disease was as odd as it was vicious, skipping the frail while victimizing the young and healthy, often leaving them desperately ill or dead within 24 hours.

Soon it had jumped the oceans and became a world-wide problem, eventually claiming over 20 million lives. It reached the United States in early September, first surfacing in epidemic proportions in eastern Massachusetts. Within the month it had swept the entire country, hitting northeastern Montana in late September. The usual control methods applied by the various health authorities were unavailing.

By mid-November, the influenza had spread into the rural areas, no doubt carried by people who had flocked into the towns and cities to celebrate the Armistice. In the little town of Wolf Point, a man brought his deceased wife to the morgue, he found six bodies awaiting burial. In the farming community east of Geraldine, Lulu's mother, Roba Cottrell, was run ragged nursing neighbors but somehow escaped getting the disease. Tragedy struck hard in Arthur's family, however, when little Opal, age nine, succumbed to the disease. Doctors in Montana were in short supply due to the war, and the State Board of Health wired the U.S. Surgeon General for help. Eight physicians were provided by the U.S. Health Service. In addition, doctors from the less hard-hit areas of the state were asked to make themselves available for relief wherever needed. The American Red Cross Nursing Service responded with seven nurses, while local Red Cross chapters provided valuable assistance. Reported cases of influenza in the state neared 40,000 with deaths more than 3,000 for the months of October through December. That amounted to more than twice the average mortality rate.

Fortunately, both Arthur and Cecil were spared influenza and were in reasonably good health to join in the joyous celebration when an Armistice was signed on November 11. At eleven o'clock on that day in a railroad car in the Campiegne Forest, somber Germans inked the agreement. Two days earlier the Kaiser had fled to Holland, there to spend the remaining 23 years of his life in seclusion. Some Allied leaders had been demanding unconditional surrender, while the exhausted Germans assumed that peace would be made in terms of Wilson's Fourteen Points. So ended the world's longest war. The Yanks had come in late but fought well. It had been a bitter and enormously bloody business, but the job had been done and the democracies, it seemed, had prevailed. For Arthur's generation, it would always be their war, the Great War, undiminished in significance by the later titanic struggle with the dictators and the forces of the Rising Sun.

In Paris the Yanks got a wild reception and the boys from Montana in the 91st Division sang their state song as they paraded through the Arc de Triumphe. In the time before they embarked for home, the soldiers were kept busy in various ways, including the holding of athletic events. That gave Cecil the opportunity to excel. From company champion runner he worked his way up to the divisional contest. Then came the day of the decisive 440 and he was ready. This was going to be the race of his lifetime, to determine who was swiftest among some 20,000 men. He stayed among the fron-trunners during most of the race and then, with a final burst of speed, he was first across the finish line! How his heart pounded and his lungs ached but how sweet the moment of victory! Then—here was the stern-faced man most every doughboy knew, Gen. John J. Pershing, stepping out of the stands to pin a medal on the boy from Kansas, which would become a truly prized possession.

Going home was, of course, the big thing. Like more than a million other soldiers, Arthur and Cecil [who never met in Europe] were thinking about family and the gladness of reunion. Arthur was anxious to see his homestead and a certain young lady he had left in Montana. Unfortunately, he was assigned to an old freighter that barely made headway across the Atlantic. The old tub rocked and rolled during a seemingly interminable voyage that left many soldiers seasick and staying close to their bunks. Finally, after 13 days, there was New York Harbor and the Statue of Liberty sym-bolizing everything for which they had been away. Tomorrow or the next day, the shouts would die away and the people would begin to forget, but for the moment how good and glorious it was to be home!

Arthur's travel was paid back to Fort Benton but he was schedul-ed to be mustered out at Cheyenne, Wyoming. His honorable discharge noted the major battles in which he was involved, no wounds received, and an honest and faithful character. That bit of paper would stay with him for the rest of his life. From Cheyenne he entrained for Fort Smith, Kansas, to visit home before returning to Montana. He was anxious to see his folks, though his visit would be weighted with sadness over Opal's passing. Her brief years on earth had been plagued with tragedy, with the ghastly burns in early childhood and then taken by the flu. The little farm Ab and Mame now called home was outside of town and when Arthur reached a small river some hundred yards from the house, he found he would either have to wade knee deep or call for a horse. His shout brought Mame running and hardly touching the ground. Soon Harold brought a horse and Arthur was with his family for the first time in five years. Mame's cup overflowed and he could not contain his tears. Here were all the familiar sights and smells of home, which brought back a flood of feeling, imparting a sense of security and peace.

The younger children almost seemed like strangers. What a dif-ference five years could make! Flossie was now sixteen and filling out

Bertha & Bert Bingaman

Arthur Henderson

Lulu Cottrell

Mr. Nance, Roba Mary, Arthur
with tame antelope

into young womanhood. Harley was thirteen and favoring his mother in appearance and temperament. He would become the preacher she wanted in the family. Harold was seven and, like the others, somewhat awestruck by this older brother returned from a far distant land. They fingered his uniform and Harold wanted to try on his puttees and hat. Ab came in from the field for supper and hugged his son with big brawny arms, while tears slid down his face and disappeared in a bushy beard. Mame thought that her boy looked undernourished and piled his plate accordingly. Her cooking was everything Arthur had remembered and he was loathe to leave the table. "This is the first real meal I've had in a long time," he nodded with evident satisfaction, "but I've eaten so much I'm about to bust." Mame beamed her pleasure and was willing to take the risk.

Outside Kansas was showing signs of spring. Father and son stood on the porch observing evidences of renewing life and listening to the soothing sounds of the river. Somewhere a meadow lark was trilling the world to rest. Ab towered beside Arthur and, resting a hand on his shoulder, reckoned that it looked like rain. For a moment, the younger Henderson remembered all of the rain in France the past year and the cold, slimy mud of the trenches and how he had never wanted to see it rain again. But this was Kansas and rain was the gift of life and the promise of the harvest. "Yes," he agreed, "it sure does" and then added quietly, "Pa, you don't know what it means to be home again."

They talked long into the evening about news from Montana and shared their grief over Opal's passing. She was the second child Ab and Mame had buried. Arthur recalled what a scourge the flu had been at the front. Ab was unsettled by her death and was thinking about going back to the section of land near Thayer. It was a lot of land but there was a small house on the place for a hired man. Claude and Clara had lived there before going to Montana. Arthur learned that Cecil would soon be arriving and that he had written to Claude and made final the transfer of the homestead. Cecil planned to go back to Montana for a while, but doubted that he would stay. Never a farmer at heart, he was thinking about getting a job on the railroad. He still carried several large brown spots on his body from the gas poisoning but otherwise was fine.

All the family slept soundly that night, tired by the late hours and excitement of Arthur's visit. They even missed a big thunder storm and cloud burst. Ab was roused long after his customary hour of rising by the excited shouts of a neighbor boy on a horse outside. "Get up! The river is out of its banks! You'll have to hurry!" Ab looked out and noticed first that the sky was clear. The river was overflowing some, but he didn't reckon that it would rise any more. There was no call for panic, even if that had been his nature, and he decided to stay put. Arthur was also awakened by the commotion and, as father and son watched the river race by, they agreed that they had gotten the predicted rain.

"I sure missed it," Arthur grinned. "I must have really been tired because I didn't hear a thing. Say, this river reminds me of the old Pottawatomie we used to swim in years ago."

"It's called the Little Osage," Ab observed. "It isn't big enough to do much damage, but there is good river bottom along its banks. It makes for good crops if you don't get flooded out."

There was healing as well as happiness in the two weeks Arthur stayed with his folks. He talked some about the war, mostly in answer to questions, but he felt the tensions and the tragedies of that now distant scene subsiding in the peace and quiet of this little Kansas farm. Planting time was coming, however, and there was a homestead in Montana that needed his attention. It was tempting to linger with his family and at Mame's table, but there was much to be done and Arthur was never one to postpone the inevitable. Besides, he was getting anxious to pick up where he had left off some 15 months before. That included renewing acquaintances with a certain brown-eyed lady. So for the second time he entrained for Fort Benton, this time, he thought, with a better idea of what lay ahead.

THE WILL TO HOLD ON

Montana homesteaders in the spring of 1919 were still putting in a wheat crop but more in desperation than out of hope. The drought that by then had overspread the northern plains kept a searing breath upon the land and little grew. Along with the drought came the grasshoppers and gophers and prairie fires devouring what little could be raised. The record yield in Chouteau County that year was nine bushels of wheat per acre. Most farmers harvested far less, around two or three bushels. 1920 brought the unrelenting winds, completing nature's seemingly vindictive treatment of the hapless homesteader. Dust storms, born in part of deep plowing, darkened the skies at noon and piled up dirt and debris against solitary shacks and sheds on the treeless prairie. The ground cracked open and pleaded futilely for water, while the homesteader and his family looked in vain for anything green. His wife did persevere with a few chickens and a marginal garden which kept starvation from the door.

Once they had sung:

> Forty miles from water
> Forty miles from wood
> We've come to old Montana
> And we're staying here for good.

But for many the will to hold on was waning. Hopelessly in debt, abandoning machinery in the fields, they were loading what little they had left into wagons and old Model T's or huddling in an empty freight car. There had to be greener pastures somewhere. In the process of their leave-taking, some 20 percent of the state's farms would be vacated.

Coupled with the drought was the post-war depression with rapidly declining prices [wheat below $1.25 per bushel], diminishing markets, and vanishing credit. Banks had multiplied during the good years, duplicating services not only in the cities but in the small homestead towns. Now they were closing by the scores. The state superintendent of banks complained that so many banks were going "busted" that he couldn't keep track of them. Stillwater County, for instance, had had 13 and was now down to 1. Chouteau County went from 17 to 5. By mid-decade more than 200 commercial banks would disappear in a flood of bankruptcies unequaled in the nation. Montana more than other states stood at the great divide. Various economic developments had fueled a population increase from under 40,000 in 1880 to nearly 550,000 in 1920. Now, however, the collapse of the homestead frontier seemed to signal very uncertain years ahead. So it was not in the best of times that Arthur returned to his adopted land.

He had counted on a change of clothes when he got home, but someone had broken into his shack and stolen everything wearable. Dismayed by the prospect, he still would have to make due with his uniform until he could afford something else. Otherwise, the homestead seemed to have fared all right under Claude's care. His brother had even plowed up some more acres in response to wartime appeals for food. He had also tried to work Bert's and Bertha's old place, but that proved to be too much and it reverted to the government.

Arthur noted with approval the improvements Claude had made to Cecil's homestead. He had patched up the cabin and plastered the walls to make it a bit more livable during the winter months. He had added a root cellar under the floor and built a barn. His attempts, however, to find a suitable well were unsuccessful and he was still hauling drinking water from the McCardle place. Claude's family had also expanded. He and Clara now had three children.

Soon after getting back, Arthur rode over to the Cottrell farm. Lulu's family had been having it hard. They had moved to Montana to find better opportunities for the four sons; however, Lorin, the second boy had died of a ruptured appendix in the spring of 1917, and

Glenn, the oldest, was one of the 934 Montanans who did not come back from the war. The Cottrell home was still kind of a social center. The house was larger than most in the area and could accommodate small dances. They pushed back the furniture, rolled up the rugs, tuned the fiddle, or got out some cylinder records for the phonograph. They also had a piano. Hawarden women sometimes met there for their "literaries" when they recited poems, gave readings, read skits, or engaged in lively debates on issues of the day. On other occasions, spell downs, card parties, pie and box socials, and birthday celebrations provided the happy times along the hard road they had to travel.

Seeing Lulu again confirmed Arthur's growing suspicion that he was not meant for permanent bachelorhood. He was nearly 28 and yet he was bothered by the thought that he had so little of worldly goods to offer a wife. It was a warm day for May as they rode "Buster" and "Maude" and Arthur explained that he would be going to North Dakota to find work in the wheat harvest. It was too late to put in a crop here, even if it were not so dry, and besides, he needed to make some money. He had not been able to save much from his meager pay as a private for Uncle Sam. A neighbor was moving his horses and cattle to Power's Lake for better pasture and had asked Arthur to help him transport his livestock. Once there, he could find more work than was available around Geraldine. Next spring he hoped that things would be better and he would be able to take up farming again. He left unspoken his hopes of what might happen after that. But the girl with the winsome smile riding beside him probably guessed.

Arthur and his neighbor loaded three freight cars with livestock and machinery and had an uneventful trip to Power's Lake, which was not far from the state line. He then found a job in the wheat harvest for $40 a month and, when the threshing was over, he hired on feeding cattle for the winter. It proved to be a severe one with a lot of snow and cold. Farmers ran short of feed and were forced to buy hay from Minnesota which had been cut from slough flats and was heavy with frozen mud. It sold for $40 a ton, which was more than a cow was worth. There was no way a farmer could make out feeding two or three tons of such poor stuff to a cow during the winter. Snow blocked the roads most of the time and the only way into town was by horseback. By early spring Arthur was ready to take his chances back on the homestead. For better or for worse, he would get some planting done.

The drought would continue into the new decade. 1921 brought a little improvement in moisture and a crop of some two million bushels for farmers in the Fort Benton area. With the market fluctuating around 80 cents to a dollar, the determined ones were hanging on and that was about all. It would be the mid-twenties before the drought lifted for a few years. Meanwhile, the great exodus continued, until some 60,000 in all had left the state.

There were, of course, various reasons why the Arthur Hendersons stayed. Perhaps most important was that he had been reared to the soil and seasoned in the bad times and the good. You learned to take the long view that encompassed the cycles of wet and dry. Nature still held your hopes hostage, but you learned to make do. Sooner or later, it would rain again, and wheat would ripple in the summer breeze, delighting the weary eye, and so you held on. It was the kind of courage bred of adversity that produced endurance and kept hope alive.

Another kind of homesteader was recently from the old country where land, generation in and out, was the privilege of the few. So he and his wife were determined in this new country to do or die to keep a place they could pass on to their children. The very meaning of life was wrapped up in having one's own soil. That opened up the future, grim though the struggle might be. Bertha's and Willie's neighbors, the Sigfred Andersons, were a good example. Immigrating from Sweden in 1904, they had lived first in Pennsylvania where he worked in steel mills until his health gave out. He headed west for Arizona in the spring of 1912, but chanced to meet on the train a man from Geraldine who convinced him to homestead in Montana.

Anderson filed on some land near a lake, figuring that the ducks would help keep his family in meat. His wife and children joined him in June of that year and he gradually expanded his shack to accommodate a family of ten children. A large garden kept the root cellar full, while pigs provided the principal source of meat. Mrs. Anderson excelled in "making do" in clothing for her family. Flour sacks were not only good for towels but for underclothes as well. Often, however, when the Anderson girls bent over in play, they advertised "Stanford Mills" or "Rex Flour" on their bottoms! But the Sigfred Andersons held on throughout the grim times and the original homestead remains in the family today.

Arthur never seriously considered going back to Kansas, even when all of his family did return. The homestead was his, and with all of the people leaving, more land could be had for back taxes. Besides, there was Lulu. He still had little to offer her by way of material comforts but decided it was time to see what she would say. So he invited her to the big Fourth of July celebration that year of 1920. Hard times did not keep the farm families in the Hawarden district east of Geraldine from having their picnics and celebrations. They had been getting together for such occasions since first coming to the area. Summer picnics would attract 100 people or more who stayed all day. Water was trucked in for gallons of lemonade and sometimes that great treat, homemade ice cream, was enjoyed by all. There was visiting and games for young and old.

But the big occasion in the summer of 1920 was the Fourth of July celebration at Arrow Creek, complete with rodeo. Lumber was hauled in for a large dance floor constructed near a clump of trees. During the day, in addition to the rodeo events, there were games like baseball and horseshoes and races and, also, a boxing match between Claude and Arthur McCardle. Claude had to be talked into doing it. He had put on the gloves with brother Arthur back in Kansas, but neighbor McCardle was another matter. Not only did he have an advantage in height and reach, but he had done considerable boxing back in Wisconsin. McCardle agreed to take it easy on Claude and pretend to be hitting him hard. As it happened during the practice session, Claude got in a few licks of his own. Later, they pleased the crowd with a rather convincing performance.

McCardle's talents ran in other directions and that evening he helped to provide music. He often played the fiddle for area dances. The night was warm but no one minded as numerous couples, including Arthur and Lulu, whirled around the improvised floor. Dancing was not one of Arthur's accomplishments, but he liked the idea of having Lulu so close and somehow managed to keep in step. What he really had in mind was the ride home and what he was going to say to this nineteen-year-old girl in his arms.

The night over Chouteau County somehow seemed different, the stars closer, the smell of hay sweeter, as they headed their horses toward the Cottrell place. The excitement Arthur felt almost made the evening air chill. His heart raced as he suggested that they dismount and walk for a bit. Soon his arm drew her close and then they were sitting on a knoll. It was not their first kiss, but Arthur trembled as their lips touched. She was more relaxed as she laid back, resting her head in his lap. "Lulu," he breathed, "you know I haven't got much, but I'll do my best if you'll be my wife. Will you marry me?" She drew his head down and pressed her lips on his. Then . . . "Does that answer you?"

The surge of relief and happiness was unlike anything he had known. Finally he found words to ask when she would like to be married. Lulu didn't help matters by smiling sweetly, "How soon do you want to get married?" Neither saw any point in a long courtship and settled on a date in early October. That would give Arthur some time to spruce up his place. As it happened, they splurged on the wedding and took a train to Great Falls where they were married on October 9th in the Presbyterian Church. Luther and Amy combined the wedding with an outing to the big city and stood up with them.

They had left their wagon at the Square Butte depot, and on the way home, passed a neighbor taking a load of wheat to town. He knew of their marriage and decided some of his 80 cent produce would be a good substitute for rice and so showered them. The big celebration came when they got to the Cottrell farm where they were greeted by an enthusiastic charivari.

Members of the family and neighbors vied with one another in the banging of kettles and the blowing of horns. Now and then the boom of a shotgun punctuated the din. After things settled down, there were refreshments and then a dance that lasted way into the night. As on the colonial frontier, guests expected the newlyweds to stay with the celebration to the wee hours.

Arthur and Lulu spent a few days with her family and then accepted Claude's invitation to stay on his place while he and his family went back to Kansas for a visit. It turned out to be all winter, and that gave them not only warmer quarters but more time to improve on Arthur's cabin. He had built it with a slant roof and now decided to double its size and have a peaked roof complete with shingles. The inside received a more homelike look and Arthur invested in a new stove with oven. His bride would not lack the means to bake, boil, fry, and can. Aside from the cabin project, he stayed busy with his livestock and Claude's and found odd jobs around Geraldine.

The town had peaked in prosperity and was now on the downside with the hard times. The census for that year, 1920, showed 354 within the town limits, off considerably from a year or two earlier. Geraldine had qualified as a second-class school district at the beginning of 1919, which meant a minimum population of 1000 within the town and its environs. But 1919 had been a real disaster for the farmers and ranchers and so for the townspeople. Wheat was scarce and selling for less than one dollar a bushel, while beef was being unloaded for eight to twelve cents a pound. Along Main Street the offices of the professional people were being closed, and in 1921 the resident doctor left town. After that it was a matter of catching a doctor from Great Falls during his weekly visit. Dentists and lawyers and the like also sought greener pastures. Geraldine residents with cars now had to find professional services in the larger towns. More significant for the economy was the closing of the Montana Bank in 1923.

All over the homestead frontier, the Geraldines had dreamed of enduring prominence and prosperity. Surely, the coming of the railroads guaranteed that. But by the early twenties those hopes had been abandoned in the face of drought and depression. Boarded-up windows and neglected fences became the symbols of inexorable change in American life which would only accelerate with the passing years. Rural Montanans were caught in the double grip of the urban movement and a stagnant population. Montana was the only state in the union to lose people during the twenties and to remain virtually static between the wars. Geraldine hung on better than most homestead towns, which became little more than an old elevator and post office-store at the place where dirt roads ran in from the spaceless plains.

A lingering hope from the great days was that Geraldine might become the seat for a new county. That would mean a courthouse and continuing prominence, not to mention more money in town. Talk had started back in 1913 when the Milwaukee laid rails through southern Chouteau County and people began questioning the long wagon ride to Fort Benton. That was about the time that the county-splitting movement was gaining momentum elsewhere in the central and eastern parts of the state. In addition to Chouteau County, other "biggies" which came in for special attention were Teton, Valley, Cascade, Fergus, Dawson, Yellowstone, Rosebud, and Custer. In 1915 an impusive legislature in the Leighton Act gave the counties almost *carte blanche* to subdivide as they wished.

An effort early in 1919 to create "Highwood County" by legislative enactment was stymied by opposition and then abandoned in the face of poor crops. By July of the following year, however, the new county movement had revived and brought in Dan McKay, the veteran county-splitter with some eighteen campaigns behind him. Under his high-pressure leadership, meetings, picnics, and dances were held to whip up enthusiasm for what would be called "Banner County". The threat of legislation prohibiting further county splitting was headed off by making the effective date of such a law May 1, 1921, leaving sufficient time for the vote on the proposed county. There was much politicizing as to the boundaries and one contemporary described the frenzied campaigning as "somewhat like war games." Finally, the division petition was ready with the required signatures for presentation to the county commissioners on November 29, 1920. It was accepted and the vote was scheduled for March 29, 1921.

Apparently, the proponents concluded that Banner County was "in the bag" and began celebrating in verse as well as preparing to select the county seat. One rhymster rejoiced:

> No more to Benton we will go,
> Our taxes for to pay,
> But bank our money here at home
> All for a "rainy day"....

> Then hurrah for Banner County
> May her land with oil float,
> Hurrah we say, do not delay
> But come and cast your vote.

Geraldine supporters assumed, of course, that "home" meant their town but a challenge came from the people of Denton and that provided further campaigning.

A county convention held on January 21, 1921, turned its attention to drawing up a slate of officers to serve the new county. *The Geraldine Review* boasted that the new county represented the best of Chouteau County and the famous wheat lands of the Judith Basin. So sure were the proponents of the outcome that a Livingston business man who had recently bought the Geraldine Flour Mills renamed his property Banner Mills. And a restaurant in town also became Banner Cafe.

The anti-divisionist forces, however, had not given up the struggle. Centered in the area's other two towns of Square Butte and Coffee Creek, they pressed their case against the self-serving interests of Geraldine and Denton. They found support, of course, in Fort Benton which had seen Chouteau County, once Montana's largest and roughly the size of Maine, whittled down by one division after another. The anti-divisionists excoriated the promoters for pushing a new county that was too large and unwieldly and would saddle hard-pressed taxpayers with further unnecessary burdens. They promised to carry the struggle "over the prairie and valleys" until "all interested shall hear the truth." However, their attempt to get a court injunction to halt matters was unsuccessful and the vote took place as scheduled on March 29, 1921.

The divisionists won handily, 1705 to 509, and proceeded to elect officials for Banner County. But their rejoicing was short-lived, for the Montana Supreme Court upheld objections that there had been improper notice of the meeting with the commissioners the previous November 29th. The Court also rejected a petition for a rehearing and so, to the dismay of its many supporters, Banner County died in birth. A rather premature map depicting Banner as part of the Treasure State didn't sell well either in Geraldine or Fort Benton. But if the divisionists lost out in Geraldine country, they were generally successful elsewhere in the state, doubling the number of counties to the present 56 and leaving a legacy of problems in management and finance.

Arthur and Lulu were more or less bystanders in the great county-splitting debate. He saw the convenience of having a county seat closer at hand and she attended a literary or two where the topic was argued. They voted for Banner but were not crushed when it failed. Of more immediate concern was their new life together. Lulu's cheerful ways and warm embrace reassured Arthur of the wisdom of the big move he had made. Claude's house was cozy and warm and he had left a generous supply of vegetables and canned produce in the root cellar. His barn backed up to a cliff and had thick sod walls and a sturdy protective roof where cows could be milked in relative comfort. The horses usually stayed in the shelter of a gully that ran near the house and barn. To cap the happiness of those first months, Arthur learned early in the new year that he would become a father in August.

March brought Claude and family back from Kansas. Arthur met them at the depot in Geraldine, while Lulu stayed home and prepared a big meal for her new in-laws. After dinner talk flowed about the folks back home. Ab and Mame had resettled on the section of land near Thayer and still had three children at home—Flossie, 18, Harley, 15, and Harold 8. Lulu was anxious to learn more about Arthur's family. She knew that with the hard times a trip to Kansas was out of the question. As a matter of fact, it would be 1945 before she was able to visit Arthur's old home and meet a then aged Ab and Mame.

Claude had found Kansas considerably more appealing than drought stricken Montana and hinted that he was thinking of returning. He had borrowed all he could on his homestead and, unless conditions improved, he would have to let the bank take it and move. Clara and the three children just needed more security. As it happened, Claude stayed on his homestead for the better part of another year, and then moved to Libby where he worked in lumber camps. In 1923, like so many others whose dreams had dimmed, he gave up on Montana and returned to his native state.

Meanwhile, with Claude back, Arthur and Lulu moved to his homestead where they would live for the next seven years. He supplemented what little farming he could do by continuing to work on area ranches, while Lulu raised chickens, hogs, turkeys, and tended to a sizeable garden. The spring on their place was no good for drinking but did help in keeping things watered. During the dry years, for many Montana farm families, the garden and chickens and cows were the margin for survival. In August, Roba Mary, named for Lulu's mother, joined the family.

Arthur's happiness was dampened by Amy's and Luke's announcement that they were going back to Kansas. They had come in 1910, in the vanguard of the homestead movement, when hopes were high and record harvests were taken for granted. Their family had grown to five children, while Luther had become a successful farmer and leading citizen. He served on the school board, promoted a Sunday School organization, and otherwise contributed to community betterment. But in addition to the prolonged drought, health had become a concern for both of them. Amy's borderline consumption was not helped by Montana's severe winters, and she worried about blizzards that isolated her and other members of the family from medical attention. Then Luke's normally robust health seemed to be failing. He lacked energy and during the cold months developed a persistent cough.

One day in late summer he came in from blighted fields and brought matters to a head. "Amy, I like this country," he began, "and I'm proud of what we've done with this place, but I've about given up on farming. So little grows here any more. Besides, the cold weather is bothering both of us. Your face, I've noticed, is beginning to show the strain".

Amy, at 34, was not about to admit that she was aging prematurely and good-naturedly reminded Luke that he was no spring-chicken. But she agreed that to stay on in Montana would likely shorten their days. The Kansas climate had been good for her during her childhood and was probably the place for them.

The decision reached, they were anxious to relocate before winter set in. So they made arrangements to dispose of the place and then had a big sale to get rid of everything but the bare necessities. They planned to stay with Ab and Mame for a while, and after that Luke figured that he could buy what he needed to start up farming again. Their farewell party brought friends from all over the area. When most had left, a somber Arthur struggled with his good-bye. In his mind was that day back in 1914 when Luke and Amy had made him and Bert feel at home in this new country. In a way they were, for him, Montana—they personified the homestead frontier—and now they were going . . . back home. Claude would be going, too. Bertha would likely stay, but that night as Arthur drove back to his place, he felt very lonesome, despite the consoling presence of Lulu by his side.

Brother Fred drove Luke and family to Fort Benton where they entrained for Thayer, Kansas, and what they hoped would be better health for them and many more years together. Amy did improve and Luke seemed somewhat better for a while. Their sixth child was born and then the seventh in early 1924. But by then Luke was flat on his back, beyond medical help, and biding his time. From his bed he watched Amy care for the infants and the older children come and go. When he could no longer speak, his eyes still conveyed a certain gladness in this circle of life and love he would soon leave behind. An autopsy revealed cancer of the liver.

Among Arthur's neighbors who stayed on despite hard times was one John Liberty who had a shack on Arrow Creek. Actually, John was a man of simple tastes who neither expected nor sought much from life. He and friend Charley Dosssett had come to Montana from South Dakota with a string of good horses and two sod plows. Their services were in demand and after a while Charley had saved enough money for a wife and a cabin of his own. John was not the marrying kind. Tall and spare, he accentuated an Icobod Crane appearance with a stovepipe hat and swallowtail coat. Thin face and steel-gray eyes completed a rather unforgettable figure. Understandably, he was sometimes the butt of course humor. One day before they parted company, John and Charley were in a saloon and a loudmouth shouted something derogatory across the room. John confronted him and when the loudmouth swung, he ducked and then knocked him to the floor. Undiscouraged, he came at John again who this time floored him with a resounding blow. The fight was over.

Arthur McCardle stopped at John's place one day when he and son Leon were on their way to Arrow Creek for a load of wood. He invited them in and they got their first glimpse of an all-purpose shack. The bed was wide enough for John and his four dogs. Several boxes at the foot were topped by a smaller one filled with straw where his favorite hen laid her eggs.

Other chickens were in a six foot pen on the south side of the shack. The sod structure had a dirt floor and heavy door made of inch boards. The bottom had a twelve inch board on hinges so that the dogs were free to come and go.

John was inclined to live from day to day and often was low on supplies. Arthur and Lulu and the McCardles at times took in a warm meal or left food. They strongly suspected that it was the first real meal he had had for several days. One hot summer day, Leon McCardle was at Arrow Creek and stopped at John's spring for a drink. He lifted the lid and started to draw some water when he was startled by a large snake swimming around in the spring. He went to the shack for a rake and told John about the snake. "Boy," he warned, "I know he's in there and I want him left alone. He takes care of all the bugs and mice that try to get in the spring." Leon nodded his understanding but decided to go on his way without the drink.

The winter of 1925-26 John took sick and the county authorities agreed to provide care in the Fort Benton hospital. Arthur and neighbor McCardle arranged for the transportation but when they got John to the hospital he refused to go in. "I appreciate what you fellas are trying to do," he declared, "but I can't live all cooped up behind those walls." No amount of persuasion could budge him so McCardle arranged with the county commissioners to keep John at his place during the winter for $40 a month.

In the spring he went back to his shack. One afternoon in late May he was caught out in a bad thunderstorm and didn't make it home. Arthur saw his horses in the corral with their harnesses on and knew something was wrong. John's body was found in a coulee some distance from his shack with his dogs standing guard. He was buried May 27, 1926, in the pauper's section of the Riverview Cemetery in Fort Benton. Whenever Arthur passed the abandoned shack on Arrow Creek, he pondered the solitary life that had been lived there—primitive even by homestead standards, but in John Liberty's own way—free!

With Claude and Amy gone, Arthur and Bertha tried to keep in touch as much as possible. Their places were several miles apart so visiting was left mostly for the weekends. Bertha and Willie had had a near brush with tragedy early in their marriage when daughter Viola was born in the fall of 1916. As with little Arthur back in Kansas, she had another difficult birth. A delayed delivery and the threat of complications put her in the Fort Benton hospital where the doctor could keep a close watch. One day he told Bertha that her tissues were retaining too much fluid and poison could be building up in her system. He had a drug which was sometimes successful in inducing the labor, but there was the danger of complications that could take the baby's life and even hers. Bertha had done enough midwifing to know what toxemia could mean and decided she really had no choice and asked for the drug. After a few tense hours, the contractions began and Viola came in a normal delivery. But that experience ended having any more children.

Bertha missed Amy. She had helped in the births of all of her children and the two sisters had stayed close. But she was too much of a social body to be lonesome. There was an active Sunday School that met in Clear Lake schoolhouse three miles from their place and she and Willie were mainstays. Often as many as 40 or 50 people would come. On occasion the Methodist minister from Geraldine would hold services, followed by a pot luck supper.

The drought dried up the lake on the elder Cartwright's land, but there seemed to be enough hay for a number of cows. Fortunately, Willie's deep well held out during the dry years. Bertha had a large garden and canned everything she could get her hands on. They raised a lot of chickens and turkeys. Each autumn the family looked forward to butchering the turkeys and taking them to market in Great Falls. That was the annual excursion no one wanted to miss.

Willie and his father had developed adjoining homesteads and then in the spring of 1925 the elder Cartwright passed away. After a while, Mrs. Cartwright moved in with her son and family and part of her place was converted to a wash house. Willie invested in a washing machine that was run by a pump engine and he also bought a stove to heat water. One morning when Arthur was visiting, Bertha asked him to go to the other house and start a fire and heat some water. After he left, the stove either threw a spark or the pipe got too hot, for as Bertha was walking toward the house with an armload of clothes she saw smoke and then flames. There was a breeze blowing and within a half-hour the place was in ashes, including some cherished furniture and lifetime possessions. Such calamities were a constant threat where houses were flimsy and water was scarce.

Willie and Bertha seemed to be firmly rooted in Montana soil, but toward the end of the decade, her health was failing and the doctor strongly advised a change of climate. They held on, however, until 1933 when Willie turned his place over to a neighbor and took his family to Thayer, Kansas. Of all the Hendersons who had sought the land of opportunity in the high plains, Arthur alone remained. Each departure weighed upon him. All his folks were now back in Kansas, but he knew that he was in Montana to stay. His family grew with the birth of a son, Robert, in 1923, and then two more girls by the end of the decade.

LIFE ON THE FRINGE

For the country generally, the coming of the 1920's had sounded an uncertain note. The great crusade to make the world safe for democracy had ended in disillusion, its leader now an ailing recluse in the White House, more and more out of touch with America's changing mood. The politics of peace had given away to the politics of normalcy, as proclaimed by the handsome Republican candidate for the presidency. "America's present need," Senator Warren Harding of Ohio affirmed in Boston in May, 1920, "is not heroics, but healing; not nostrums, but normalcy; . . . not surgery, but serenity; . . . not experiment, but equipoise; not submergence in internationality, but sustainment of triumphant nationality." That sounded good to many Americans including most veterans who had had enough of the Old World and its cynical leaders and interminable problems. Harding won in a landslide.

But wartime passions were not easily resolved into serenity and equipoise. Americans had grown accustomed to hating the "Hun" and despising the "slacker". Now animosities were focused on a variety of people—Negroes, Jews, Catholics, foreigners generally, radicals, strikers, Bolshevik sympathizers. Numerous strikes during 1919 involved more than 4,000,000 workers while the "red summer" of that year saw the worst race riots to date. The contagion of fear bred belief in many that a Communist takeover was imminent in the United States.

Such fears were fed by a rash of bombings. The anarchists involved were few in number, but their provocative needs generated a wide hysteria and an atmosphere that was hostile to dissent. Attorney-General A. Mitchell Palmer rounded up some 6000 suspects, many of whom proved not to be aliens and over one-third of whom were later released. Eventually 556 were deported. In the growing anti-foreign mood, Congress abandoned the historic open door policy in 1921, and enacted a highly restrictive quota system for immigrants. The mood, too, was the background for the controversial Sacco-Vanzetti trial of 1920. The two Italian immigrants, confessed anarchists, were arrested for the murders of a factory paymaster and his guard at South Braintree, Massachusetts. The trial and convictions resulted in strong protests that the men had been found guilty on questionable evidence and that they were actually being condemned for their political views. Legal proceedings dragged on until 1927 when Sacco and Vanzetti were electrocuted admidst cries of "the miscarriage of justice in Massachusetts."

Farmers like Arthur were less concerned with a "Red Menace" than with keeping bread and butter on the table. The postwar depression, following the collapse of the war boom, effected the country generally, leaving nearly 5 million unemployed, but an upswing in business had occurred by 1922. The farmer, however, did not share in the return of prosperous times. Gross agricultural income had fallen from 17.7 billion in 1919 to 10.5 billion in 1921. And it was only the beginning. During the 1920's farm income would drop from 15 to 9 percent of the national income. As prices and land values declined, taxes and debt grew.

The farmer had gone all out in response to wartime appeals to feed the Allies and by 1920 had increased total acreage harvested by some 15 percent over 1910. Now the export market was declining and prices at home hardly made it worthwhile to put in a crop. Wheat sold for 40 cents a bushel and would go lower, while cattle at the stockyard would drop to 5 cents a pound. The drought added to the gamble of trying to farm, while an unsympathetic administration in Washington did little for the farmer's plummeting morale. "Farmers have never made money," President Coolidge was quoted as saying. "I don't believe we can do much about it."

Agrarian discontent was voiced through the Grange and the Farmers' Union and the new American Farm Bureau Federation. Senators and congressmen from the agricultural states sought clout in a Farm Bloc, while the Progressive Party in the Election of 1924 espoused the farmers' cause. Magazines like the *Farm Journal, Wallace's Farmer,* and *Kapper's Farmer* kept the countryside posted on efforts in Congress to pass beneficial legislation. But these efforts were unavailing when President Coolidge twice vetoed the McNary-Haugen Bill.

Around Geraldine, as elsewhere, farmers had little good to say about the government, state or federal. When Arthur and his neighbors gathered, sooner or later the conversation drifted to politics. Their engrained individualism made them wary of government programs, but they were willing to go along with almost anything in order to survive. Meanwhile, they and their families still ate because they had cows to milk, hogs, turkeys and chickens to butcher, and a large garden to supply vegetables for the table and to fill the root cellar. Odd jobs provided a few dollars for other necessities. Turkeys and butter were also marketed for cash.

Farm wives like Lulu kept their big boilers busy, canning just about everything they could get their hands on. Vegetables like corn and peas which were more difficult to preserve were usually dried and then put in cans or fruit jars. The County Extension Service was helpful in explaining better ways to process fruits and vegetables and meats. Chicken was the main meat item during the summer, while hogs and beef cattle were butchered in the fall for winter consumption. What couldn't be cured or canned was eaten right away. Hogs contributed most to the menu as hams, bacon, chops, sausage, and lard which was used for various purposes, including pie crusts. Canned beef was also tasty and added to the more skimpy wintertime meals. When the canning season was over, wives like Lulu might celebrate their accomplishment by splurging 25 cents or so on a house dress at Penny's.

Aside from drought, economic distress, and a sense of political powerlessness, the Arthur Hendersons were also a part of a dwindling rural America. By 1920, for the first time, more people lived in cities of 2500 and more population than on the countryside. Once, in Jefferson's America, the rural part had counted for 95 percent. By 1960 two-thirds of population would be living in urban communities. The cities were the centers of the new prosperity, spearheaded by the flourishing automobile industry, the rise of chemical manufacturing, and the phenomenal growth of the radio and motion picture businesses. The cities were also the places where the new morality challenged traditional values and zany fads and fashions competed for the headlines. If urban writers pictured the aridness of rural America, many country folk were convinced of the sinfulness of city life.

One evidence of the tension between urban and rural America during the 1920's was the revival and spectacular growth of the Ku Klux Klan. Strong in the rural areas, the revived Klan was founded in Georgia in 1915 and, after some changes in leadership, was boasting a membership of 5 million by 1923. In Montana the Klan had an estimated membership of 6000. One observer recalled seeing 1000 Klansmen parade down Higgins Avenue in Missoula in 1925. The Klan's influence was especially evident in school elections around the state and in the withdrawal of proposed legislation in 1927 to provide free textbooks for parochial schools. In Billings, the presence of the Klan was seen in a full page advertisement in the *Gazette* proclaiming Klan principles and by a burning cross from time to time on the Rims.

Scandal in high places in 1925 dealt the Klan a body blow and thereafter its numbers and influence waned. A more profound and enduring impact upon rural Montana came with the automobile, the radio, and the movies. Of the 8 million cars on the road in 1920, a few were rambling around Geraldine, mostly Model T's. Even at Henry Ford's low prices (a Model T sold for around $300), a car was beyond Arthur's means. It was against his nature to do what the majority of owners were doing and to buy one on the installment plan. Some of his neighbors who had an automobile still took the horse and wagon when they wanted to be sure of their destination. Poor or nonexistent roads were not to be taken lightly. Balled up gumbo under the car or sticking to the wheels required periodic stops for cleaning and took the joy out of an afternoon's ride. Hills could also present a problem, unless the owner of a Model T discovered it had more power in reverse and resorted to backing up the steeper grades.

By 1924 Ford was selling 51 percent of the vehicles made in the country. Not only was his Model T priced to sell, but it proved to be a versatile machine for the countryside. Its narrow tires were good for the prairie, while farmers soon learned how to jack up the hind wheels and attach a pully for various power needs. Some farmers around Geraldine, however, made more substantial investments in heavier cars like the Maxwell and the Willys-Knight. The Willys had a seven passenger model which was ideal for taking a large family on a picnic to the mountains or on a day's excursion to Fort Benton for a Fourth of July celebration or a political rally.

One of Arthur's neighbors had invested in a new car but wasn't quite ready to abandon his horses as a means of getting around. He decided that his wife should be the operator. The salesman in Great Falls had given detailed instructions, but when she tried to back out of the barn, she couldn't remember which pedals to use. She was afraid to touch anything for fear of running forward and damaging both vehicle and barn. Her husband was no help, until he solved the dilemma by hitching a horse to the rear bumper and pulling the mystery car out of the barn. The story soon made the rounds, to the amusement of farmers like Arthur who still had to depend on horse power.

By 1925, the number of automobiles on the road had more than tripled to 17 million. Improvements such as the self-starter and enclosing the cars made driving more pleasurable and enhanced America's love affair with the automobile. Its impact was great upon rural society in providing easier access to town and also in the weakening of family ties and the traditional values of country life. As the new decade came, Arthur capitulated to changing times and acquired his own Model T.

The radio was another powerful agent of change in rural living. The first commercial radio station went on the air in 1920 and in a few months a new craze was sweeping the nation. Within two years Americans were spending more than 60 million dollars on radio equipment and the amount soared to 430 million by 1925. Geraldine had a radio store by 1922 and was advertising repair services for most models. $50 Crosleys and Atwater Kents were popular makes and were soon showing up in more and more homes in the area. The more inventive could experiment with a do-it-yourself mail-order kit.

The farmer with the radio found his popularity high, especially on those evenings when boxing matches were being broadcast. Neighbors flocked in, undeterred by the cold ride home on a winter's night. The improbable title fight in Shelby on July 4, 1923, between champion Jack Dempsey and challenger Tommy Gibbons made rural Montana more fight-conscious. Shelby, however, paid dearly for its brief moment in the spotlight. The town about went broke paying for the ill-conceived venture.

Radio programming grew apace, providing a wide variety of entertainment. Rural Montanans like Americans everywhere could twist the dial for news and sports casts, coverage of political campaigns, Sunday sermons, songs by Rudy Vallee or the beat of jazz musicians who had made their way to Chicago from New Orleans. Until the state got its own stations, Montanans were dependent on places like Denver and often the reception was poor and limited to the evening hours. Farmers who invested in radios had to hurry the evening milking if they wanted to get in on the shows. By the time Arthur and Lulu were able to buy a radio, the reception was much more reliable through stations like KFBB in Great Falls.

Motion pictures came out of the war years with longer films and more ingenious plots and featuring stars to captivate audiences around the land. Mary Pickford was America's first "sweetheart". But then came comedians like Charlie Chaplin and Buster Keaton, cowboys like Montana's own Bill Harte, sophisticated and wicked women like Gloria Swanson and Theda Bara, and foremost for the female audiences, the "great lover", Rudolph Valentino. The transition to sound towards the end of the decade brought great anticipation and millions of movie-goers sighed in relief when they found that Greta Garbo could really talk. By that time an estimated 95 million customers a week were going to the theatre.

Geraldine had a theater or two, but they didn't last very long. Arthur and Lulu drove over to Fort Benton for a very occasional visit to the movies. On those times, however, the hard realities of everyday existence could be forgotten for the moment in the world of imagination and romance. The movies, along with the radio, accentuated the ambivalence in feeling about a city-oriented culture. Rural Ameica tended to view the urban centers as sinful and overly materialistic, but at the same time was fascinated by the luxuries and excitement of city life coming over the air and portrayed on the screen. Underneath, there was a quickening tempo of change that disturbed the more traditionally-oriented countryside.

Farm families like the Hendersons kept fairly abreast of current events. Towns like Geraldine had a weekly newspaper, and there were the larger publications, like the *Fergus County Argus* in Lewistown that was delivered three times a week. Lulu read *Woman's World* and *Household* and there was also *The Saturday Evening Post*. The telephone was pretty much limited to the towns, although here and there enterprising farmers strung out their own line. The "system" consisted of insulators mounted on two by fours attached to fence posts with the wire powered by drycell batteries. The line ran into the nearest town where messages could be relayed to and from the Bell System.

A "general ring" [long ring] was the signal for everyone to listen in for some important farm news. In this way some rural Montanans first heard about the signing of the Armistice, the death of President Harding in 1923, or Lindbergh's celebrated flight across the Atlantic in May of 1927. The last event joined city and countryside in the adulation of a hero the decade so badly needed. And Montanans proudly noted that "Lucky Lindy" had lived for a while in Billings. Geraldine was served by the Northern Montana Telephone Company, but farmers like Arthur were too far out to benefit.

Farm families did not lack for entertainment. There was usually music available for listening of dancing, with victrolas, player-pianos, or the radio. The square dance on Saturday evening at the school or the community hall featured a fiddler who sometimes became an institution in the area. During the summer, picnics could be a big thing. The Hawarden Picnic was held each year in June on the Saturday closest to the 16th. Begun in 1915, it drew families from all around. One hundred people and more joined in day-long activities and consumed gallons of lemonade and ice cream. Arthur and Lulu always tried to be there.

Living out of town did make it difficult to keep up church connections. Arthur had been raised a Baptist, while Lulu's background was Methodist. She was the more active in church affairs. When weather permitted, a preacher from Geraldine would hold services in the school house and during the summer Sunday School workers would conduct classes there. Occasionally, Arthur and Lulu timed a trip into town to attend a special program at the Methodist Church. One such visit was to hear Professor Fred Kelser's glee club from Intermountain Union College. The school in Helena had built quite a reputation for its music program and also for its debate teams which traveled widely around the country. Intermountain was also known and appreciated as a place where young people with limited training could prepare for college and then go on to get a baccalaureate degree. Intermountain maintained an academy which opened the way for many older students with only an 8th grade education. Arthur could appreciate what the college was trying to do for the young people of the region.

Intermountain had an unusual background which began in territorial days over in Deer Lodge. There, on March 30, 1878, some concerned citizens met at the courthouse to consider establishing a college. The venture was backed by such prominent Montanans as William A. Clark, Samuel T. Hauser, and Conrad Kohrs. The Montana Collegiate Institute opened in the autumn of that year with three faculty and two dozen students meeting in some rented rooms. By 1882, it was decided that the little school would fare better under religious auspices, so control was shifted to the Presbyterians who were evidencing considerable interest in education on the frontier. The name was changed to the College of Montana and opened for business in 1883 under the presidency of Reverend D. J. McMillan of Salt Lake City. Significant for the future was his assurance that the school would not be narrowly denominational but open to young people of broadly Christian background. By 1889, the college could boast three brick buildings and 160 students with 12 faculty members. But the struggle to survive was complicated by the Panic of 1893 and the opening of the Montana university system which drew off both students and faculty.

The doors closed in June of 1900, and soon empty halls with broken windows stood as forlorn symbols of a dream that had failed in the beautiful Deer Lodge Valley. In 1902 a man who would become prominent in Montana educational and political circles was called from Iowa to be the local superintendent of schools. The vacant campus bothered Ernest Eaton, as did the educational needs of many young people in the rural areas. He persuaded his brother, Lewis, another educator in Iowa, to come to Deer Lodge and join in a venture to be called the Montana College and School of Manual Arts. They leased the buildings in 1904 and soon had enough students in attendance so that the Presbyterians decided to resume control again in 1907. The Eatons moved to Billings to pursue their dreams and there, with the help of concerned citizens, incorporated the Billings Polytechnic Institute in 1908. The Deer Lodge school struggled on and then closed its doors for the last time in 1916. Its few remaining assets were later transferred to Intermountain.

The Methodists were also early in expressing a concern for education on the Montana frontier. At the first annual session of the Montana Conference in Bozeman in August of 1877, a committee was appointed, including the Rev. W. W. VanOrsdel and Gov. Benjamin F. Potts, to investigate the establishment of a school. Among the motivations was a desire to provide a place of learning so that Methodists would desist in the "pernicious habit" of sending their children to Romish schools. Evidently no great urgency was felt, for it was not until 1888, at the conference in Missoula, that action was finally taken to establish an institution of higher learning. With the pretentious name of Montana University, the little school opened outside of Helena in the Prickly Pear Valley in 1890. Later by state request, the name was changed to Montana Wesleyan College. The Panic of 1893 was also devastating here. That fall the president and faculty were expecting an enrollment of 130 but found themselves at the opening assembly looking at seven, six of whom were expecting financial aid!

For the next four years, two determined staff members carried on a preparatory academy and then the board of trustees resumed control. They moved the school into town and then followed two decades of continued struggle and some growth, with Montana Wesleyan maturing into a full-fledged four-year college. Its graduates included the ministers of many Montana churches, like the one in Geraldine. Much credit belonged to faithful teachers like Paul M. Adams and to strong supporters like Rev. William VanOrsdel. "Brother Van", as he was known around the state and a legend in his own lifetime, scoured the region for financial aid, promoting $50 scholarships for young people to attend his beloved school. His colleagues in the ministry, living on a pittance, dug deep to give what help they could. If untiring effort and the power of prayer could keep Wesleyan open, Brother Van would surely see to that.

Arthur and Lulu thought of him that evening as they sat in the church he had helped to organize in Geraldine back in 1913. It was one of a hundred or more that Brother Van had planted as District Superintendent and which would stand over the years as symbols to his boundless energies and undiminished faith. The young man from Gettysburg who arrived at Fort Benton in 1872 in response to his own Macedonian Call left unnumbered friends in all walks of life, the humble and the highly placed, when he passed on at Great Falls in December of 1919.

In 1923, Montana Wesleyan and the defunct College of Montana merged into Intermountain Union. That institution grew and survived the ordeal of the Great Depression, only to be dealt a fatal blow by the earthquakes in Helena in 1935. The last and most destructive came on October 31st. A new but poorly built gymnasium was damaged beyond repair and other buildings were badly cracked. Operations were shifted to Great Falls where the Methodist Church and the Deaconess Hospital provided facilities. The community was not especially receptive to the college remaining there as Great Falls already had a Roman Catholic academy. So the next year Intermountain accepted an invitation to relocate on the campus of the Billings Polytechnic Institute. There the schools co-existed until they merged as Rocky Mountain College in 1947.

The glee club from Intermountain left no one disappointed and Arthur and Lulu were glad that they had driven in. During the summer especially, their days were long, from sun up to dark, leaving little time or energy for anything but work. Arthur was anxious to obtain a larger farm and took every opportunity to work out for wages. Some places he could earn $70 a month and with their frugality they were able to put some money aside. There was plenty of land available for back taxes. The state legislature had passed a bill that permitted counties to delay payment of taxes for five years and many homesteaders had taken advantage of it. Some never intended to pay and others couldn't, so the county had to take the land. Some counties reclaimed up to 20 percent of the land during the hard times of the 1920's and 1930's, and of course, wanted to get it back on the tax rolls. County officials were glad to grant title for back taxes, or, if there were no takers, they would deal on a dollar or two per acre. Arthur intended to acquire more land and have a more efficient operation.

Meanwhile, his family was growing with the addition of a daughter, Luella, on December 13, 1926. Roba Mary was now five and little Robert was tagging behind him in the barnyard. Arthur was grateful for Lulu's sturdy health, for sisters Amy and Bertha certainly had their problems. At times, when he thought of Bertha, his gaze wandered to Square Butte and he would think of Bert in agony on the frozen ground. That seemed so long ago and yet the pain of loss lingered on. Arthur would frown as he pondered the unfairness of life. At other times he missed Cecil and his fun ways and Claude working the homestead next door. Leon McCardle had taken that over for one dollar an acre, and later he would move Claude's cabin to his own place where in combination with a discarded schoolhouse he was able to fashion a rather spacious domicile.

The Henderson cabin, though expanded, was crowded with the three children. Also Roba Mary would be starting school next year. Arthur valued the memories of this place he had homesteaded back in 1914, but realized it was time to relocate closer in, nearer to a school. Fortunately, the Hicks place was available for rent, eleven miles east of Geraldine, and early in 1927, he moved his family there.

The winter of 1926-27 had been an unusually mild one, so much so that the folks in Great Falls held a straw hat parade on April 1 in observance of the "winterless winter" that was now past. That day they got the only snow to speak of for the season. And from then on it turned wet. The 4th of July Celebration in Fort Benton was rained out. Many visitors had to spend the night in the high school gym and auditorium and didn't mind it a bit! Arthur's wheat and barley turned out real good on his new half-section. Roba Mary was enjoying making friends at South Shine Lake School, while Lulu was appreciating more ample living quarters. The two-story house with three bedrooms, livingroom, and kitchen was a vast improvement over Arthur's homestead shack. Being seven miles closer in also afforded better access to Geraldine.

1928 was also a good crop year and Arthur began looking around for a larger farm. He found a place for rent four miles north of Graceville with 460 acres and moved his family there the next year. By now he had acquired a fair number of horses and livestock and farm implements. At Graceville, buoyed by the improvement in weather, he made the big move into the machine age with the purchase of a Fordson tractor. As for many farmers, though, it would take a while in the way he felt to make the transition from the only source of power he had known since his boyhood in Kansas.

The small farmer with a few horses had much more than an impersonal relationship with them. They had names and each one possessed a different disposition. There was appreciation and affection for the team that worked well in harness, each horse compensating for the other's shortcomngs. They could be counted upon to get the job done. The death of a good horse somehow diminished the farmer and his family. It was, therefore, no small thing for the Hendersons to make the transition to the machine age. Arthur continued to work horses around his farm and, of course, old Buster's place was secure for as long as he could last.

In December, 1929, Lulu gave birth to their fourth child and they named their daughter for Bertha. Soon it was apparent that the infant had both serious digestive and respiratory problems. The lungs were not functioning properly and food was not being digested. The little body weakened and in three days the baby was gone. Lulu's anguish was not quite the same as that of a new mother with empty arms, for she had three children at home. Still, each one was precious and unique and through her tears she could only trust that little Bertha was better off in an eternal home.

That October the long-heralded prosperity of the 1920's collapsed in the paroxysms of Black Thursday. Desperate attempts to prop up the stock exchange failed as Americans, grown accustomed to profits upon profits, shook their heads in disbelief. In the weeks and months that followed, despite assurances from high places, it was clear that the country was in deep trouble. It was evident that Mr. Hoover's prophesy along the campaign trail was grieviously mistaken, for the poor house was not about to disappear from the land. By the spring of 1930, at least four million Americans were unemployed and soup kitchens in the large cities were serving long lines of sullen men for the first time since the recession following the war.

The coming of the Great Depression, as it would be called, was less traumatic for the Arthur Hendersons than for the city dwellers. The farmers had grown accustomed to hard times and would see no substantial and long term improvement in his way of life until the coming of another world war. Depression dropped prices further until it was debatable if one should bother with a crop. After you paid for storage, you might be lucky to get 20 cents for a bushel of wheat. Weatherwise, some years were better than others. 1932 saw good crops, despite destructive hail storms ("the great white combine") in the area. Chouteau County was leading in wheat production with an average of 4 million bushels. The new administration was beginning to talk new programs to prop up prices. So the flame of hope flickered and the Arthur Hendersons hung on.

In fact, Arthur was ready for his own place. He had allowed the old homestead to go for taxes and now wanted his own land again. He and Lulu had scrimped and saved, worked out and sold turkeys and butter, and had enough put aside for a half-section. They heard of a place at Flat Creek 15 miles northeast of Geraldine and rode over to see it. The tract was 240 acres, but there was an adjoining 160 that could be added later for less than one dollar an acre. The four-room shack didn't excite Lulu, but it was larger than their original one and had several windows and the walls were sealed tight enough to keep out the weather. It would do until they could improve upon it.

Lulu scrutinized the chicken house while Arthur eyed the land around. He noted that to the west it dipped slightly to accommodate Flat Creek while to the south it lifted gradually to meet Haystack Butte in the distance. An old cavalry trail angled across the property. All in all, Arthur thought the place had possibilities. And there was a school within walking distance for the children. So they rode into Geraldine and bought the farm for $600. It was the beginning of a wheat ranch that would eventually encompass over 1700 acres.

The fall of 1933 Roba Mary went into Geraldine to live with her grandparents and attend high school. Robert and Luella disdained walking for the fun of riding his pony to school. What else could an aspiring cowboy be expected to do? The animal was gentle enough, but adventuresome Bob insisted upon leaving the well-beaten path and jumping his pony over ditches and boulders and the like. Luella seemed willing to put up with her brother's wild ways, but often she arrived home with torn clothes and badly in need of the wash basin. The situation reminded Lulu of her own school days when she rode a pony and pulled her sisters in a cart. That cart, she mused, must still be in the family and could be handy again.

She mentioned the matter to Arthur one evening and they decided to ride over the next Sunday to the Cottrell place and see what had become of the cart. It was still there and proved to be repairable. So Lulu was spared unnecessary sewing while Luella was afforded a less hazardous mode of transportation to school.

With the approach of winter, fuel was always a concern and Arthur and friend Frank Owen decided to find some coal. Frank had the reputation of being one of the best well diggers in the county and he also claimed to know something about mining. He had discovered a fourteen inch vein of coal on a cliff above the Missouri River and was sure that he and Arthur could meet their fuel needs without too much effort. Since trees along the Old Muddy were free, they assumed that coal could be considered in the same category.

So they fashioned a coal car out of old lumber from a deserted homestead. Wheels with a beveled edge were taken from two discarded binders. The country was full of old machinery left by settlers who had lost their places and had moved on. The track was made from two by fours set the appropriate distance apart and edged with strips of iron. When all was ready, the two enterprising farmers discovered that mining was fast and relatively easy. But it wasn't long before word got around and the river bank was crowded with amateur miners. Later the government decided to put a price on the resource and Arthur and Frank turned back to wood. Both had good horses and wagons and timber was fairly close. Besides, they reasoned, wood was a cleaner fuel and the women really preferred it.

One Friday in January of 1934, Arthur went to town to bring Roba Mary home for the weekend. She complained of feeling sick, weak, feverish, and nauseated. She felt better after supper and the next day helped her mother with the house cleaning. Sunday she was ill again but wanted to go back to school. Arthur and Lulu packed her things and took their daughter into Geraldine. By the time they arrived, she was feverish and seemed so deathly sick that Arthur called the doctor. He took a blood test and then telephoned Fort Benton for confirmation of his findings. She had appendicitis and would have to be taken to the hospital the next day.

She felt better after the doctor left and managed some supper. Daughter and parents went to bed early to be rested for the next day, and all was well until nearly daybreak when Roba Mary awoke with a high fever and groaning with excrutiating pain. Arthur called the doctor who hurried to rent a car and they hastened toward Fort Benton. Lulu rode in front while Arthur let his daughter rest her head against his shoulders. Outside of town, she suddenly slumped over in her father's arms. The doctor stopped the car and got in back to see what had happened. Blood drained from his face as he looked up, faltered, and said, "She's dead!"

The shock was overwhelming, bringing panic and disbelief. How could it be that their happy and healthy Roba Mary lay so silent beside them? Death was no stranger, but this was so sudden and so wrong. One could come to terms with little Bertha's brief stay, but a thousand associations of everyday life had made Roba Mary a part of their very being. How could a righteous God permit such a thing to happen?

Lulu found some solace in her parents' understanding. They had buried a son, also dead of a ruptured appendix, and had seen another not return from war. Arthur remembered his mother standing beside her youngest son's grave and quoting Job: "Naked I came from my mother's womb, and naked shall I return; the Lord gave, and the Lord has taken away; blessed be the name of the Lord." Faith helped, but mostly the grieving parents instinctively buried themselves in work, with whatever could keep their hands busy. The long wakeful hours of the night were the hardest when the vagrant "what ifs" robbed them of rest and the forgetfulness of sleep. Time alone would be the healer, the balm of the Eternal's care. Meanwhile, new life was stirring again in Lulu's body and on November 6, 1934, Joyce Lillian joined the Henderson family and it once more numbered five.

ADJUSTMENT AND CHANGE

It had been twenty years since Arthur's arrival in Montana and a period of unprecedented change. The world of his young manhood had been by and large a hopeful time, but then came the "Great War" and all too soon the "Great Depression". He had joined in the last massive westward migration only to see the homestead frontier collapse in the face of drought and hard times. Many homesteaders had been oversold on the region and its promise. Many were educated people but ignorant of farming in the semi-arid Plains. Abandoned machinery rusting in the fields, losing the battle with the elements, reminded Arthur that nothing was to be taken for granted in wrestling a livelihood from this land. The blighted prairies of the 1930's underscored that point. Yet, the same wisdom told him that in time it would rain once more and the fields would again lie golden with ripened wheat, barley, and oats.

He was also aware of developments that during his years of farming would revolutionize the agricultural scene. Farm technology and agricultural science, along with changes in farm organization and marketing, would do much to shape the future. Technology and agricultural science would make farming vastly more efficient, but would also aggravate the problem of excess supply and depressed prices. They would contribute to the movement toward fewer and larger farms. Farms would peak at 6.8 million in 1935 but by 1950 were down to 5.6 million. They eventually bottomed out at around 2.4 million. In 1981, the number of farms in the United States increased slightly for the first time since 1935.

The most significant single factor in farm technology was replacing the horse or mule with the tractor. Ponderous steam-driven machines had been in use on large farms since the 1870's, but the small, general-purpose gasoline tractor came along during and after the war. There were some 85,000 in use in 1918. The replacement of the cleated metal wheels with pneumatic tires in the early 1930's was another significant improvement, affording greater speed, less fuel consumption, and longer wear. By the time that Arthur bought his Fordson there were upwards to one million tractors on the farms of the nation. There were, also, since the war some seven and a half million fewer horses and mules.

Arthur, like the other small farmers, was no longer limited by the hours he could work his horses. Substituting a fresh team at midday, he could at best get in nine or ten hours. With his tractor and three plows he could cover four or five times as much land from sunup to dark. Further, he could get more done when the soil was right for cultivation. This was especially true when he exchanged the Fordson for a heavier International. With fewer horses he needed less pasture land and less of a hay crop and so could plant more wheat and barley. This had an offsetting disadvantage in times of surplus crops and depressed prices. The tractor also represented a substantial investment and costs for fuel and repairs. Sometimes when his plows bogged down in rough ground and he had to shut down for frequent adjustments, he wondered if he was not better off with horses. That problem would eventually be solved with the hydraulic lift. Clearly, though, the future belonged to the tractor and mechanized operations.

Changes in farm implements had also carried agriculture a long way since John Deere's steel plow and Cyrus McCormick's pioneer reaper made wheat growing feasible in the West. The plowing, hoeing, planting, and harvesting operations had been further mechanized with disc plowing in place of the deepcutting moldboard plow, with duck-foot cultivators and improved toolbars, soil packers, drill presses, and harvesting machinery. By Arthur's day the combined harvester-thresher, cutting and threshing in one operation, was saving the farmer almost as much time and effort as his tractor. And he could increase significantly his production of wheat per acre.

Along with his tractor, Arthur also bought a Ford truck which helped in his hauling and marketing operations. With less land needed for horses, he and Lulu expanded their garden and turkey business and had more produce to market in Geraldine and Fort Benton. Trucks were about as popular with the farmers as were tractors. By 1930, there were some 900,000 on America's farms. Few were sold during the hard times of the Great Depression, but then the number in use doubled in the 1940's.

Aside from mechanization, the Hendersons were benefitting from better land practices, especially concerning moisture and soil conservation. Moisture was utterly critical in dryland farming. Earlier a system of land tillage called summer fallow had moved down from Canada and was being found useful by Montana wheat growers. This involved alternate fallowing and planting with the fallow land plowed and cultivated several times during the summer so that rain could permeate the soil. Moisture would be retained for winter wheat planted in September and would carry over to the next year. The experience with summer fallow was generally good in Montana and eventually nearly all wheat growers would adopt it.

The loosening of the soil, however, did result during the dry and windy 1930's in fields blowing away. That led to the adoption of another land practice from Canada, namely, strip farming. Wheat growers began to cultivate their fields crossways to the prevailing winds and following the natural contours of the land in strips of planted and unplanted land. The Roosevelt Administration encouraged this practice with a subsidy of 50 cents an acre for strip-farmed land. The new method proved to be effective and Montana became one of the most strip-farmed states in the nation.

Valuable help in farming came to the Arthur Hendersons from the Montana Extension Service and Montana State College experiment stations. Through bulletins, meetings, and demonstrations they learned about land utilization, production costs, marketing techniques, and new varieties of wheat more resistant to drought, winter kill, and disease. In particular, they benefitted from the work of Professor Milburn L. Wilson and his associates at Bozeman. Wilson was regarded as the country's foremost authority on dryland farming. In fact, he had been invited to visit Soviet Russia to advise on the monumental farm problems there. He had postponed his trip, however, to direct another railroad traveling exhibit in Montana. He had been doing this each winter to acquaint wheat growers with the latest in technology and farm management. That year of 1929 when the tour reached Great Falls, Arthur drove over to see the exhibits.

Wilson urged Montana wheat growers to aim at a minimum 10,000 bushel production to have an efficient operation. That meant at least 800 acres, preferably more, and also adequate mechanization to keep production costs at acceptable levels. On his experimental farms around the state, he and his fellow researchers had demonstrated how it could be done. Arthur was impressed and returned to his Flat Creek holdings determined to add acres as rapidly as resources allowed.

It was evident, however, that even with efficient production methods the farmer was in a losing battle. Too many circumstances were beyond his control. Major concerns over market, falling prices, mortgage foreclosures called for action at the federal government level and little had been forthcoming during the 1920's. The Hoover administration in 1929 did encourage Congress through the Agricultural Marketing Act to establish a Federal Farm Board to stabilize farm prices by withholding temporary crop surpluses from the market. The Board also tried unsuccessfully on a voluntary basis to get farmers to curtail production. But too many farmers feared that others wouldn't play the game and planted as much or more than before. That experience would help convince the incoming administration that price supports needed production controls to be effective. For the remainder of his term, President Hoover continued to oppose such an approach and help for the farmer was minimal.

Meanwhile, agrarian unrest was turning into revolt. In desperation farmers watched their net income spiral downward until in 1932 it was one-third of what it had been three years before. In Iowa, an old agrarian crusader named Milo Reno started the Farmers' Holiday Association to hold produce off the market until prices rose to acceptable levels. With clubs and pitchforks grim-faced agrarians intercepted trucks bound for market. Elsewhere farmers dumped milk, used their corn crops for fuel, and resisted foreclosure proceedings. Friends and neighbors descended upon auction sales, scared off the outsiders, and bought back at a pittance the farmer's land, implements, and stock for him. In Iowa, an uncooperative judge was dragged from his bench, beaten, and threatened with the hangman's noose. Continued violence brought out the National Guard and scores of protestors were arrested.

Montana farmers were less inclined to revolt. The Farmer's Holiday Association was active in the state, but didn't get much accomplished. In the Northeast corner, around Plentywood, some of the more alienated organized a Communist group and published a newspaper called the *Producers News*. More Montana farmers joined the Farm Bureau or the National Farmers' Union which had become leading advocates for agrarian justice in the state. The Bureau was on the downside, while the Union was coming on strong and during the mid-1930's, had considerable influence in the legislature. The Grange also helped to channel the farmers' anger and despair.

Arthur noted on his trips into Geraldine other witnesses to the deepening depression—more empty storefronts along Main Street and more men riding the rails as the trains passed through town. At some depots, he had heard, homeless men were sleeping on the floor, curled close to the pot-bellied stove to keep warm. At the Laurel yards, outside of Billings, a "jungle" had sprung up to accommodate hundreds of unemployed riding Northern Pacific and Great Northern freight trains. Montana, like the rest of the nation, waited impatiently and wondered what the new president could do.

Roosevelt dealt first with the banking crisis, but soon turned to the farmers' plight. He had picked as his Secretary of Agriculture Henry A. Wallace, from one of the country's leading farm families. Three generations of Wallaces had provided leadership, with Henry's father having served as Secretary of Agriculture under President Harding. Wallace turned to another farm authority, a man he had known in college, Montana's Milburn L. Wilson to help in the formulation of a new program. Wilson played an important role in planning the Agricultural Adjustment Administration which went into operation in 1933. In a variety of ways, the AAA sought to raise farm prices by limiting surpluses, including direct payments to farmers who cooperated in curtailing crop acreages.

The AAA's impact upon Montana wheat farmers was evidenced in price increases before the year was out, with wheat bringing 70 cents a bushel at Fort Benton. "It was," recorded a local journalist, "the first bright note in three years." In the following four years AAA made some 140,000 contract agreements with Montana farmers bringing upwards to $10 million into the state. Equally urgent with farm prices was the matter of foreclosures and Roosevelt acted in late March of 1933 to establish the Farm Credit Administration. With powers confirmed by the Congress, the FCA moved quickly to refinance farm mortgages, and in the process obliged creditors to accept less than the 10 percent they had been demanding. $100 million was loaned out in the country during the first seven months, and Montana farmers would get some $78 million over the next five years.

The Taylor Grazing Act of 1934 was not of immediate concern to

Arthur, but he had worked on enough ranches in the region to appreciate its significance. Responsible stockmen had sought for some means of controlled cooperative grazing on the public domain. Successful experimentation with a cooperative grazing district in southeastern Montana led to legislative approval in 1933 and influenced the Taylor Act of 1934. Sponsored by Congressman Edward Taylor of Colorado and urged by both Wallace and Secretary of Interior Harold Ickes, the measure aimed at conservation while limiting cattle production and giving the stockman a firm lease arrangement on pastureland.

Young men in Geraldine country, as elsewhere, were interested in the Civilian Conservation Corps as an opportunity to earn while learning job skills working on range and forest lands. CCC "soldiers" were required to send money home to help their "folks", but there was enough left over to ride into the nearest town on Saturday night and have a good time. Farmers and others needing income took advantage of the Works Progress Administration to work on county roads and various projects, the most ambitious of which was the Fort Peck Dam. Pushed hard by the New Deal, that project at its peak in 1936 employed more than 10,000 workers and merited coverage in the first issue of *Life* magazine in November of that year. Another enduring legacy were the windbreakers planted by CCC and WPA workers to help control soil erosion. All in all, during the 1930's the New Deal pumped more than half a billion dollars in Montana. With a static population of about 550,000, that meant $1,000 for every man, woman, and child! Only one other state did better.

Beyond the control of legislation were the recurrent droughts of the 1930's. Conditions varied in different localities, but droughts were general and devastating during 1934, 1936, and 1937. Fierce winds whipped across parched fields, depositing precious topsoil on neighboring land. The new superintendent of the Congregational conference marveled at how afflicted farmers could joke about conditions, one suggesting to another that he would have to raise the wheat that year since all the topsoil was now on his side of the fence. "Just wait until tomorrow," the reply would come. "The wind will shift and you'll get yours back and mine, too!"

Dust was everywhere and most women learned to live with it. More perfectionist types swept and dusted in quiet desperation, unyielding in the dreary futility of their task. The garden and a geranium or two, kept growing with grim determination, provided a bit of green to rest the eye and to gladden the weary spirit. Abandoned shacks filled with dirt, Russian thistles hung up on fences, and the ground cracked open for lack of moisture in a scene so desolate that the meadowlarks almost forgot to sing.

To add to the farmer's woe, 1935 and 1936 brought the greatest scourge of grasshoppers and Mormon crickets to date. The grasshoppers came in their airborne migrations to descend upon everything green, devouring crops and stripping the trees of their leaves. The farmers fought back by poisoning the wheat in order to kill the marauders. Mormon crickets moved along like black molasses covering up to one mile a day and leaving a path of destruction. Swarming across highways, they made driving hazardous and their crushed bodies gave off a peculiar odor. The Geraldine area was especially hard hit by the crickets, and Arthur attended meetings to learn about the most effective means of combatting the menace. Hand and mobile arsenic spray guns were used. Also, holes and ditches were dug, edged with low tin fences and filled with oil. When the crickets fell in, they were burned. Such measures proved to be effective in the area, but the Mormon crickets swarmed elsewhere in the State. South of Billings in 1938, there was an infestation from the Pryors that was stopped short of the city. Nature cooperated in diminishing the problem thereafter.

The Red Cross was committed to helping those who stayed on their farms and worked with dwindling resources to alleviate the misery of the hard times. Local volunteers gave generously of their time and efforts. Beyond such help it was a matter of resourcefulness and sheer determination not to be dried or choked out. Many farm families ground whole wheat in the coffee grinder for breakfast food and found it to be surprisingly good. Those with feed grinders also made a course grade of flour and baked their bread. Clothing was an equal challenge, as pants and dresses wore thin and the wife longed for some stout jeans material. Patches multiplied and she became a wonder in "making do." Even a new house dress at 25 cents was only an occasional luxury.

The minister or priest who served in the farm belt during the hard years felt keenly the Biblical admonition "Comfort ye, comfort ye, my people." The times were a stern test of faith, theirs as well as the people they served. Unanswered prayer called for a deeper probing of God's providential care. The "plateau pilots", as they were sometimes called, had to muster the faith and fortitude to minister to those whose hope and courage were blown about in the great dust clouds riding in on the gusty winds. They, too, lived on the margin of survival in cold, spartan parsonages, thankful for a square meal, rattling around in old cars, risking the prairie elements to reach some preaching station, sharing a common bond of privation with those they served. For some of their flock, the adversity was too great to believe any more in the goodness of God. Others did not lose their faith, but they were reluctant to attend a church they could no longer support for lack of money.

Churches, like banks, had sprung up around the country during the good years. Many little homestead towns witnessed the keen rivalry to be first on the scene and to attract the largest congregation. For the Protestants, it was said that the first train into town carried the Methodist District Superintendent, the Presbyterian Synodical Executive, and the Congregational State Superintendent. The Methodist generally rode the "cow-catcher" to be first off and to grab the best church site. Who ever got off first, many towns were as "overchurched" as "overbanked" and the coming of hard times made for painful adjustments.

Fortunately, by 1929, a growing spirit of cooperation had brought forth the Montana Missions Council. That body encouraged exchanges of property and consolidations of churches wherever indicated. Methodists might take over in one town and the Congregationalists in another. Sometimes pride in denomination died slowly as when in Malta a Congregational minister moved in and the Methodists hung tough on the name of the new church—Methodist Congregational Church. The church founded by Brother Van in Geraldine remained Methodist, with the only other church in town being St. Margaret's Roman Catholic. The two were quite adequate for a population of 300 or so living in the community in 1930.

For those who endured the hard years, it was in large measure a matter of living one day at a time. One could only be overwhelmed by brooding about the future. Adversity couldn't be faced all at once. Each day's burden was enough to bear. The hard times caused many to leave, but in others, they brought out the best, a sculpturing of character that tempered patience with hope and bolstered the will to see things through.

From the country at large, as the depression deepened, came the angry voices of the social prophets and the panacea seekers. For a while, Father Charles Coughlin's "Golden Hour of the Little Flower" had a larger radio audience than Amos 'n Andy. Many farmers liked the Irish priest's rolling attack upon the bankers and their "filthy gold standard" and his advocacy of an inflationary, silver-backed currency.

But it was an old country doctor living in California, Francis E.

Townshend, who, perhaps, stirred the greatest excitement on the Montana countryside and around the land. His attention was focused on the over-sixty group who had doubled in number since 1900, but his proposal had sweeping implications for the whole economy. Every citizen over 60, he argued, should receive $200 a month on the condition that it would all be spent. The "senior citizen" would be cared for and the circulating funds would re-invigorate the economy. Townshend clubs sprang up overnight around the land and the graying pied piper soon had a large and loyal following. His program failed to gain New Deal and Congressional support, but, perhaps, did have some influence in the passing of the Social Security Act in 1935. Meanwhile, his movement did provide a hot topic for the farmers around Geraldine and elsewhere.

The four-room shack on Flat Creek was filled with the activities of a growing family. Robert was now high school age and pressuring his parents for a horse. A pony no longer fitted his station in life. Besides, a neighbor had some children just right for the pony and little cart. Arthur agreed and a deal was made and young Bob was on his way to manhood. He was now ready to move into town to begin high school, to defend himself against the arrogance of upper classmen and to compete for the attention of the girls.

Arthur appreciated Bob's help about the place. He was now in his mid-forties and, though still capable of doing a hard day's work, was glad for his boy's strong and willing arms. Bob seemed to have a way with horses, and neighbors brought theirs to him to be gentled and trained. That put some change in his pockets and made him feel more independent. He already knew what he wanted in life, to follow in his father's footsteps and someday to take over the farm. So he shared fully in the work and the planning and was especially happy when he and Arthur could talk about more acres and machinery.

1938 signaled the end of the dry years. Heavy rains washed out bridges and culverts and caused local flooding in the county. That proved to be a good crop year. Prices stayed low and many farmers stored their grain. 1940 wheat production in the county soared to nearly 5 million bushels and another war in Europe would mean higher prices again. The long siege of the hard years seemed about to end. Even the grasshoppers were looking elsewhere for feed. Then in July of 1940, Lulu entered the hospital once more and gave birth to Marilyn Fay.

Her coming called for a party and some reflections. The house on Flat Creek was filled with Bob and his friends and Luella was also gathering some male admirers. She had her mother's soft brown eyes, coquetish smile, and the twist of petite shoulders that brought the boys around. Arthur viewed his family with thoughtful satisfaction. In many ways, he reflected, the years had not been kind, with the tragedies that had robbed him and Lulu of their own blood and the grim struggle to survive. But, here was new life, and the beginning of better times. Perhaps, he mused, in his Montana passage, the good would outweigh the bad.

WAR AND THE
END OF HARD TIMES

The failure at Versailles in 1919 to lay the groundwork for lasting peace was evident by the early thirties in the coming of a new age of militarism in Europe and the Far East. Instead of a world safe for democracy, there was the rising menace of new tyrannies. When the Arthur Hendersons thought about all the sacrifice in the trenches of the late war, it was hard not to be bitter and cynical and to conclude that America would be wise to stay out of Europe's messes.

This included keeping the Communists at arms' length. When Montana's newly-elected Senator Burton K. Wheeler took a trip to Russia in 1923 and came home advocating diplomatic recognition and the reopening of trade, he was denounced by many newspapers, including one in his home state that called for his deportation. Wheeler saw no reason why the English and the Germans should make all of the profit in reselling American products to the Russians. Recognition came eventually in November of 1933, but by then international trade was wracked by the Great Depression.

Peace talk in the twenties, such as the Kellogg-Briand Pact of 1928, proved to be illusory when Japan stormed into South Manchuria in September of 1931. For most Montanans and Americans generally Manchuria was at best a remote place on the map. Much more immediate and urgent was the matter of keeping bread on the table.

But as aggression spread and Japanese planes began bombing Shanghai, killing thousands of men, women, and children, anger escalated in the United States against "uncivilized warfare". Movie-goers, including Arthur and Lulu, on their occasional trips to Fort Benton, saw war brought near in the newsreels and went home resolved to boycott Japanese goods.

In January of 1933, while Americans were waiting for Franklin Roosevelt to take over a beleaguered presidency, Adolph Hitler became chancellor of the German Republic. Shortly thereafter, he was withdrawing Germany from the League of Nations and announcing a program of rearmament. Late in 1935, his fellow dictator, Benito Mussolini, sent Italian troops and planes into semi-defenseless Ethiopa. The next move was Hitler's in reoccupying the Rhineland in March of 1936—all in bold defiance of the Treaty of Versailles and of the League. Another dictator, Generalissmo Francisco Franco, was on the rise in Spain with the outbreak of civil war there that same year.

Few Americans wanted any part of old Europe's melancholy scene. Lingering postwar disillusionment was stirred by a spate of books at mid-decade sensationalizing the tremendous profits of the "blood-sucking" munitions manufacturers in the last war. Montanans looked on with interest as Senator Gerald P. Nye of neighboring North Dakota headed an investigating committee which held highly publicized meetings confirming immense profiteering. Isolationist orators assured Americans that they were forever safe behind vast ocean barriers, while the public in general approved a succession of neutrality acts passed by the Congress. Parents like Arthur and Lulu with sons like Bob coming of age took comfort in their government's stand.

Montana's outspoken Senator Wheeler had become the "premier isolationist" by the time Hitler's invasion of Poland in September of 1939 triggered the Second World War. He joined forces with such prominent citizens as Senator Nye, Henry Ford, and Charles Lindbergh to push the program of the *America First Committee* to keep the United States out of Europe. That fall and winter an ominous quiet settled over Europe, broken only by the Soviet invasion of Finland, while Hitler plotted his next moves and American correspondents talked about the "phony war". The next spring the great debate between isolationists and the interventionists began in earnest when Hitler unleashed his panzer divisions on his weak neighbors to the west and by June had overrun the famed "Maginot Line" and forced France to surrender. Following the "miracle at

Dunkirk," England stood alone.

Americans were overwhelmingly anti-dictator and many were profoundly moved by Churchill's courageous leadership and the determination of the British people to remain free. More and more shared Arthur's growing conviction, based upon memories of twenty years earlier, that the United States could not remain for long on the sidelines. Yet, in the Election of 1940, Jeannette Rankin ran on a peace ticket in Montana and was returned, after a long absence, to the House of Representatives. Wheeler and the isolationists stuck by their guns, and the senator embittered the debate with his accusations that Roosevelt was employing a smoke screen to conceal his real intentions of getting the United States into the war as soon as possible. When F.D.R. proposed the land-lease bill in January of 1941, in response to Churchill's urgent appeals for assistance, Wheeler went on radio with his oft-quoted remark that Roosevelt's war policy was like his farm policy, intent on "plowing under every fourth American boy."

Hitler's invasion of Russia in June of 1941 brought more pressure from home for the senator to change his stand. Some Montanans feared that Roosevelt would withhold defense spending in the state, while a number of labor leaders opposed his continuing isolationist views. But Wheeler remained firm until the attack on Pearl Harbor changed his mind, even as it unified the American people as little else could have done. "The only thing to do now," he declared, "is to lick the hell out of them." Only Jeannette Rankin, consistent to the end with her long-held pacifist convictions, cast the lone dissenting vote against war.

Soon the Hendersons, like millions of American families, were caught up in the anxieties and dislocations of wartime. From back in Kansas came word that Arthur's youngest brother, Harold, had enlisted and was employing his skills as a bulldozer operator in the Pacific. His was the hazardous job of laying out landing strips while enemy sharpshooters made life miserable. Iwo Jima in particular was a place he would never forget. Somehow he survived and served again in the Korean War.

Claude's son, Keith, was on a battleship that shook off a Japanese suicide plane and continued to rain shells upon the enemy. Amy's oldest son, Harold, was not as fortunate when a kamikaze pilot hit his ship and he landed in a sea of fire. Many of his buddies perished, but Harold survived to experience another ordeal, when, like another sailor who would later become president, his boat was sliced in half on a foggy night and he had a long swim before he was rescued. From that time on he served out the rest of the war on an aircraft carrier.

Harold's younger brothers, Richard and Ralph, were also in the Pacific, leapfrogging islands in the Allied strategy for conquering Japan. On one occasion, Keith and cousin Richard had several days together, and on another, Keith's ship docked where Uncle Harold was working a bulldozer. Briefly, they enjoyed a respite from the grim routine of war. Amy's youngest boy, Eugene, landed in France, while his brothers served in the Pacific, and was soon caught up in the fury of the "Battle of the Bulge", in which he was gravely wounded and would carry pieces of shrapnel for the rest of his life. Arthur's younger brother, Rolland, had a son, Carl, who was also in the army. He was part of the Allied Armada that stormed Normandy Beach, where he had a leg nearly shot away and his fighting days were over.

At the farm on Flat Creek, Robert was now eighteen, graduated from high school and wondering which branch of the service to choose. He wanted to enlist before being drafted. Arthur had tried to discuss options with his son, but somehow the words had not come. Thoughts of horrors past in the trenches of a futile war caused him to change the subject, until one day Lulu persisted that he talk things over wth Bob. That afternoon he mustered the courage and sat down with his son in the barn.

"Bob," he began, "you know how much I hate war. I can't bear the thought of you going through what I did." He paused before adding, "A lot of fellas I knew never came back."

"I know, Dad, and I'm not afraid. Besides, you were a foot soldier. I want to join the navy like Keith and Harold."

Arthur mulled over that possibility and then took another tack. "Have you thought about the merchant marine? You can't fight a war without supplies, you know."

Bob noted that a friend or two were talking up the merchant marine and, after some further conversation, father and son agreed that that was the way to go. Inwardly, Arthur felt relieved. It was a compromise that he could accept. He knew that the merchant marine was a precarious place with the U-boats sinking ships at an appalling rate, but, at least Bob would never know the horrors of trench warfare. Shortly thereafter, the younger Henderson enlisted and was gone for the duration of the war. The surrender of the Japanese found him at Okinawa.

As in the First World War, Montana's contribution to the armed forces was greater in proportion to population than that of most states, exceeding its allotted quota. Montanans were early to enlist and in large numbers. The rejection rate was low for physical reasons, below the national average, and, very interestingly, in May of 1944, Montana was one of three states reporting no rejections for illiteracy. In all, some 57,000 men and women served their country and, again, as in the earlier war, the fatality rate ran high. Montanans at home evidenced the same spirit of strong support in oversubscribing eight savings bond drives. In proportion to population, Chouteau County lead the state in bond purchases in 1942.

In addition to those in the armed forces, some 35,000 men and women left the state for the centers of war industry, creating a serious labor shortage. Many men left to work on the Alcan Highway when construction began in April of 1942. Mines and smelters were hard put to operate, while the farm crops of 1942 had to be harvested with about half of the normal crew of workers. Wages were the highest since the last war, but farmers like Arthur had to depend more and more upon machinery to get the job done.

War brought the lifting of acreage restrictions and subsequent expanded production. Chouteau County had a bumper wheat crop in 1943 that overtaxed storage and transportation facilities. Wheat acreage in the state nearly doubled during the forties as demand increased, weather in general stayed favorable, and prices climbed to over one dollar a bushel. Arthur found himself adding more acres, using more power equipment, and employing the latest methods of soil conservation. In addition to strip farming, he had learned the value of leaving wheat stubble on his summer fallow to prevent blowing soil. But with all of the improvements, as he looked around the place at Flat Creek, he realized how much he missed Bob and how anxious he was for his return.

In the evening, like most American families, the Hendersons turned on the radio to get the latest reports. Lulu also listened to the regularly scheduled news programs on KFBB Great Falls throughout the day. The war turned radio around, from an entertainment-dominated medium to one with an essential worldwide newsgathering and reporting function. Entertainment was not forgotten, but news commentators like Alex Drier, H.V. Kaltenborn, Lowell Thomas, and Edward R. Murrow now became familiar household names. Murrow's dramatic broadcasts for CBS from London during the battle of Britain made a deep impression all over the land. Radio also performed a vital service during the war in the promotion of bond sales, recruiting for the military, and carrying appeals for the Red Cross and similar causes.

Listening to the radio took a toll on the nerves during much of 1942 as most of the news was bad. German tanks were deep within Russia and smashing across North Africa toward the Suez Canal. Hitler's *Luftwaffe* was intent upon bombing Britain into submission and his submarines were destroying more Allied shipping than could be constructed. The Japanese were threatening India, Australia, and Alaska, and had China cut off except by air. The Axis powers seemed to be having things their own way.

Along with the dismal news from overseas, Americans faced a new way of life sorely restricted by shortages of almost every kind. On the one hand, they became accomplished scavengers, collecting old iron and steel, discarded aluminum utensils, tin cans, old tires, and anything else that could be reprocessed for the war effort. On the other, they were introduced to the world of rationing, to stamps for meat, sugar, coffee, and other restricted food items, and to cards limiting the purchase of gasoline. New tires were all but out of the question and one came to consider the frequency of trips in view of the thread-bare tires on the car. Kids kicked at the limit on candy bars or became patrons of various stores, while parents fussed about sugar for their coffee or tea, but generally Americans did not want for food. It was their love affair with the car that caused the most chiseling for extra gasoline and related items.

Late in the war, Montanans learned that Japan was floating bomb-balloons their way. Years earlier Japanese scientists had discovered that the westerly flowing jet stream could be used as a high altitude weapons carrier. Bombs could be landed on the American mainland, igniting forest fires, doing other damage, and precipitating panic among the people. When the tide of war began to change against Japan, the bomb balloons were put to use. Of the three hundred and forty or so that reached the United States, some thirty-five were reported to have come down in Montana, with no resulting damage. Generally, the press kept a lid on balloon incidents, in cooperation with the government's request, but a harmless bomb landing near Libby was too much for the local editor to set on and he scooped the nation with a story of what had happened. If panic was what the Japanese had expected, few Montanans or Americans elsewhere were of a mind to oblige.

Before 1942 was out, radio newscaster Gabrial Heater was finding occasion to come on the air with his cheery "Good evening!" There's good news tonight!" Colonel Jimmy Doolittle's visit over Toyoko on April 18th was a morale booster, giving Tojo and the Japanese war lords a taste of American bombs. Little damage was done in the raid and all but one of the sixteen planes later crashed or were abandoned, but the Americans had struck back and that was important. Much more significant to the course of the war was the news of the American victory at the Battle of Midway in June, 1942, which was really the beginning of the turning of the tide in the Pacific. From that point United States forces seized the initiative and island by island a determined General McArthur, backed by superior naval power, made good on his promise that "I will return."

In Europe the German advance into Russia bogged down before Stalingrad and soon the Russians were counterattacking and Stalin was calling upon his allies to open a "second front" in the west. Meanwhile, Field Marshall Rommel's *Afrika Korps* was checked at El Alamein and forced into retreat back to Tunisia. In the air, the British and Americans were launching massive attacks on Hitler's industrial centers, and by the spring of 1943, the battle against the marauding U-boats was being won. "Operation Torch" opened a second front in North Africa under the rapidly rising General Dwight "Ike" Eisenhower, intent on getting at Hitler's *Festung Europa* through the "soft underbelly" of the Mediterranean. The later fighting in Italy would prove to be some of the fiercest of the war.

D-Day on June 6, 1944, was the long-awaited big showdown with the Fuhrer's main forces. With increasing mastery of the air, the Allies relentlessly drove across France toward the Rhine. Newscasters back home mentioned places like Chateau-Thierry, Rheims, and Verdun, which brought back painful memories to the Arthur Hendersons. Hitler threw everything he had left at the Allies in the bloody Battle of the Bulge—and lost. Thereafter, it was just a question of time until his suicide in an underground bunker on April 30th of 1945 and the German surrender which followed on May 7th. The next day, V-E Day, the church bells rang from New York to Geraldine and beyond.

In the Pacific, the president's military advisers were cautioning that it would take another year and probably a million troops to subdue Japan's mainland. So a fateful decision was made by the unseasoned but resolute man in the White House. On August 6, 1945, a superfortress named *Enola Gay* hung in the sky over Hiroshima and dropped the bomb that stunned the war lords and shaped an uncertain future for humankind. When Japan still hesitated, three days later another awesome cloud of destruction rose over the city of Nagasaki with frightful loss of life, but the end was now sure. On September 2nd, on the battleship Missouri, in the bay Admiral Perry had first visited nearly a century before, General

MacArthur presided over the surrender ceremonies. And once more, back home, the church bells rang as Americans celebrated V-J Day and the end of the country's costliest war.

As in 1918, the boys were anxious to get home. Mothers, fathers, wives, and sweethearts pushed for rapid demobilization, which, as it happened, left Europe too unguarded against the remaining menace of Communism. Keith was the only Henderson who opted to make a career in the navy. Like his father, Bob was anxious to get out and put the war behind him. In temperament, he was like Arthur—quiet and not conversational—he would have little to say about his wartime experiences.

Bob got back in August and earlier that year, in February, Arthur and Lulu had taken their long-postponed trip to Kansas. Lulu had never seen Ab and Mame whose remaining years were now becoming uncertain. He was 81 and she 77. Ab had made his last move to a little house in Thayer, and it was to that destination that Arthur and Lulu and the two girls entrained from Geraldine. The old folks were still keen and enjoyed the two-week visit immensely. The intervening years since Arthur had last been there had been eventful and there was much to be shared and recalled. For father and son, there was farm talk about the unprecedented changes that had occurred since the older Henderson had first put a plow in Illinois soil. Ab passed on four years or so after that visit and Mame followed him in 1954. Arthur and Lulu were so grateful for the time they had with them.

Bob had no problems abandoning the life of the seaman for that of the farmer. He much preferred the feel of the tractor to that of a ship heading into foul weather. Farming was all that he had ever wanted to do and now he could get back to working with his father and really being himself again. The farm at Flat Creek was now a ranch and there was a big harvest to get in. Wheat looked good in the county and, despite some destructive hail that cost a million bushels, the wheat crop in the county turned out well. In the midst of the harvest, younger sister, Luella, got married and moved to Great Falls.

In one respect, Bob differed from his father. He saw no point in waiting around until you were 28 or so to get married, especially after he found a young woman who was just right for him. Ilene Bell Dawson came from a family that had homesteaded in Montana back in 1886. Her parents had a place just south of Geraldine where she had been born in 1919. She was three years [or so] older than Bob and their paths had not crossed in school. Ilene was widowed with a little boy, but Bob figured that he would be getting two for the price of one.

Housing was the next consideration, and he and Arthur found an unused school house which could be converted into rather comfortable accommodations. Fortunately, the means of relocating such buildings had improved considerably since the twenties when a team of 24 horses dragged the old Sunnyside School across the prairie to a new place. Now the school house was jacked up and set on beams with heavy wheels and pulled by trucks and tractors to the new foundation Bob and Arthur had prepared for it. With a room added, Bob was ready for matrimony and brought his bride to Flat Creek in August of 1946. Arthur and Lulu remembered the little shack they had first called home and were glad that Bob and Ilene did not have to begin married life like that.

They also reflected on other changes in farm life during their 26 years together. With the progress of the Rural Electrification Administration came the great age of convenience and the saving of old kerosene lamps for emergencies. Few New Deal measures left a more enduring legacy to rural America. By 1939, some 6,000 farms in Montana had electricity, including the ranch at Flat Creek. The Hendersons were slow to embrace the modern appliances. Lulu saw no reason to abandon her old wood cook stove that had been so dependable over the years. Among other things, she had a reputation for pies and biscuits that could be jeopardized in a needless change. Heating was another matter. A good oil furnace was as economical as any other type of fuel and far more convenient, so they converted to oil.

In 1946, new appliances were not that available anyway. It took time for industry to retool for peace and to meet the massive buildup of consumer needs during the war years. Such demand triggered an inflationary spiral which brought higher prices for whatever could be bought. An area wheat rancher vacationing in California that year had an opportunity to sell his Buick at an irresistable price. He and the Mrs. talked things over and decided to sell and take the train home. Surely he would be able to pick up another car without much trouble. At the local dealership, however, he became number ten on the list of hopefuls. Badly in need of transportation, he waited impatiently to be called. After three weeks, he went back into town to find that he was now number fifteen! After considerable "hell-raising" he paid top dollar for a stripped down Ford without even a heater.

On the ranch, Arthur still used horses for some operations,

though most required tractors. He swore by his sturdy old army truck and refused as long as possible trading it in on a late model. For Arthur, one did not easily forsake tried and true friends. Of course, he did not hang on to machinery that was always breaking down. That could be folly in plowing or harvest time. But throughout his life, he had lived by the gospel of frugality and refused to make changes just for appearance's sake.

He did not skimp on planting the best seed wheat available, and he scoured the country for good bulls and kept his best heifers for breeding. He stayed abreast of the latest soil conservation measures, improving and expanding the use of stubble fallow. After the war, notable advances in weed control came with the use of chemical sprays that killed weeds without damaging crops, preserving precious moisture for the wheat. In 1946, weed spraying was introduced into Chouteau County, and ranchers like Arthur were soon taking advantage of such methods to increase yields per acre. Along with weed control, the use of new fertilizers did much to up productivity, increasing the harvest by 6 to 8 bushels per acre. With acreage controls again likely, the grain producer could still look forward to increasing his overall production.

The handling and storage of grain was made much easier with the use of the motorized auger. Earlier, whenever the terrain permitted, ranchers had often built storage facilities on a hillside, to be able to shovel grain in on the high side and unload it on the low side. The improved auger of the 1940's and 1950's greatly expedited the process of handling grain. Another boon to the rancher was the perfecting of the hydraulic lift, providing for the mechanical adjustment of plows as the tractors moved over difficult ground.

Part of Arthur's plan in improving upon his holdings was to hedge against the return of hard times. World War II had pulled the country out of depression, but he shared with many Americans misgivings as to what would follow. He remembered only too well the economic collapse of 1920, from which the farmer never did recover until the guns boomed again in Europe. But fears faded as the economy adjusted quickly and expanded to accommodate pent-up needs for housing and all manner of consumer demands. Industrial productivity would increase over 35 percent between 1946 and 1960 when the gross national product crossed the 500 billion mark. But equally notable was the fact that agricultural productivity nearly doubled during the same period.

Grain for Europe's devastated peoples was in great demand following the war. A drive in April of 1946 to get wheat to the hungry overseas brought a solid response from the Arthur Hendersons of Chouteau County. In time, though, the foreign markets fell off and the farmer was left with his old predicament of overproduction and low profits. While the politicians debated the kind of aid he should be given, his share of the national income continued to decline.

But Arthur had been seasoned in harder times and could take satisfaction in what he and Lulu had been able to accomplish. Especially, he enjoyed having Bob to help work the ranch, and he began having thoughts of the day when he would retire and turn everything over to him. Meanwhile, father and son shared an affinity for the good earth. There were the compensations that did not show on the ledger sheet: the smell of freshly plowed soil in the springtime, the constancy of nature in producing its own—a newly born calf or a crop—in the fullness of time, the soft touch of a gentle breeze on a field of green, the sight of maturing wheat turning golden in the sunlight. There was so much in the legacy of the land, moments of sheer enjoyment, to chase away the memories of bitter disappointments and painful loss.

Bob also shared with his father-in-law an abiding affection for horses. Hobart Bell had homesteaded around Malta before moving to south of Geraldine to take over an uncle's place. Farming was a necessity to keep bread on the table, but much of Hobert's spare time was spent training and trading horses, promoting rodeos, and, when he had the opportunity, engaging in a game of polo. Bob could also ride with the best of them and enjoyed a rodeo from time to time.

1946 was a red-letter year in Chouteau County, for it marked the one hundredth anniversary of the founding of Fort Benton—Montana's "Mother Town". Folks flocked into Benton from all around, including the Hendersons, to remember the eventful life of Alexander Culbertson, agent for the American Fur Company. He had established a post up river in the winter of 1846-47, and then moved it to the location which became Fort Benton. Visitors strolled along the mile-long levee and recalled the stories of the city's heyday in the early 80's when steamboats brought goods from all over to the world's most inland port and when the streets of the bustling town were filled with a rich assortment of humanity. In 1946, Benton was growing once more, after decades of hovering between 1000 and 1200. The census for 1950 revealed a population of 1500.

Arthur was pleased when Bertha's and Willie's daughter, Viola, decided to leave Kansas and return to Montana. She missed her childhood friends around Geraldine and the land of her birth. She was much like her mother in sociability and it wasn't long before Viola claimed the affections of a young man. Leon McCardle was ambitious and intended one day to be operating a 2000 acre spread. He had once owned Cecil's and Claude's old place, adjoining Arthur's homestead. Leon and Viola were married and in time added a cozy little cabin to their place in the hope that Bertha and Willie would decide to spend their last days there.

The folks came back in 1956 and once more Willie planted his garden and Bertha canned vegetables for the long Montana winter. They were to have several years of contentment before old age took its toll. Willie suffered a stroke in December of 1965 and lingered on to the summer of 1967. Bertha was to outlive him another ten years, when in a rest home, in Fort Benton, coffee cup in her hand, she closed her eyes in eternal sleep.

RETIREMENT

As the 1950's came around, Arthur turned sixty and began to consider seriously a lessening of responsibilities. Like Ab before him, he was thinking about a smaller place of forty acres or so where he and Lulu could take life easier. He still lived by the work ethic, but his pace had slackened some and he was content to let Bob toss the hay bales and handle the heavy tools. Arthur noted that a number of his contemporaries were making the move into town or to smaller places and it seemed the wise thing to do. Bob could handle the ranch with all the machinery they had acquired. It was not like the old days when a man and his team were limited to three or four acres a day.

Familywise, it was also a good time to make the move. In June of 1952, Joyce, the next to youngest, married her girl friend's brother, Roy Bryant from Highwood. Roy was headed for the service and would make a career in the military. That left Marilyn at home and she would soon be of high school age. A location close to town would have real advantages. As a matter of fact, Arthur had been eyeing forty acres in the town of Belt which would suit their needs just fine. And Great Falls was only twenty miles away for occasional shopping trips or in case of medical emergencies.

Arthur had been sharing his thoughts with Bob and one morning in early 1953 decided to make his move. "Bob," he began as they walked toward the barn, "your Ma and I talked things over last night and we've decided on that place in Belt. You don't really need me here any more. Of course, I'll be around from time to time and can give you a hand with the harvest. But the place in Belt is far enough away so I won't be tempted to get under foot."

Bob started to say something, but the elder Henderson continued with unaccustomed loquacity. "I'll need some of the older machinery to work that forty acres and some cows and a few horses." He chuckled as he added, "Of course, your Ma will want to raise a few pigs and chickens along with her garden. She wouldn't know what to do without them."

He paused and Bob slid in a question. "Do you plan to leave soon, Dad, or wait a few months?" Never one to dally once his mind was settled Arthur indicated that they would be moving soon in order to be well settled for Marilyn to begin school in the fall. As a matter of fact, he guessed that he would change overalls after lunch and drive over to Belt and close the deal.

Once moving would have been a far simpler matter for Arthur and Lulu. Now there was an accumulation of household goods and the miscellaneous baggage of the years that required several trips from the ranch to Belt. The new house was a comfortable four-room structure, with basement and garage, well built and better than anything they had owned before. Close by was a two-room cabin suitable for guests, which over the years had housed visiting relatives and friends or a chance stranger seeking shelter for the night. Arthur soon had a garden planted and busied himself throughout the summer repairing fences and doing battle with the long-neglected crop of weeds. Many weekends he and Lulu worked in a visit to the ranch just in case Bob needed to talk something over with him.

Marilyn struggled with the volatile emotions of a new teenager, certain that she would not find again friends as tried and true as those of her childhood, yet excited about the prospect of beginning school in Belt. The community was about twice the size of Geraldine and she would be going from a rural schoolhouse to eighth grade in town. Belt was an old mining community that by report got its name from a "belted butte" mentioned in the Lewis and Clark Journals. It occupied strategic ground as a natural thoroughfare from northwestern Montana to the Judith Basin. From time immemorial buffalo had frequented the pass, while Crows and Piegans had gone that way on their horse-raiding forays against each other. Ponderous freight wagons crawled to and from the bustling trade center of

Great Falls through primarily sheep raising country. Later, the Great Northern would lay out rails rimming the town on their way to Billings. What would become Belt was little more than a stage station, store and saloon, and a blacksmith shop.

Then about 1890, P. J. Shields, wandering son of the Emerald Isle, scouted the area for his fellow countryman, Marcus Daly of Butte. The copper king figured he was paying too much for out-of-state coal and wanted more of the native ore. Mining started Belt on its way and it was a booming town of 4000 by 1894. After mining collapsed with the pullout of Anaconda in 1912, the tough-minded citizens of Belt refused to let their community become another Montana "ghost town." Many of the miners had farming backgrounds in the old country and took up homesteading. Slowly, the transition was made and Belt became the trading center for a prosperous dryland farming region. By the end of World War II, millions of bushels of wheat and 150 carloads or more of cattle were being shipped annually out of town.

The spunk of Belt people was proven again the year Arthur and Lulu came to town, when a devastating flood swept through the valley in 1953. The Hendersons liked what they saw of a deeply-rooted community spirit and determination to hang on. Once again, those who predicted that "that was the end of Belt" were proven wrong.

By fall, Lulu had the house fixed to her satisfaction and decided to take a job cooking at the high school. That left Arthur alone most of the day to follow a leisure pace in working around the place. There was always something that needed fixing, fences and corrals, and the like, but now he was not in a race against darkness or the seasons. He could stop to savor some strawberries from Lulu's patch and ponder the wisdom of being too busy to enjoy the simple gifts of life. He could fuss with his old tractor to get it running better knowing that a harvest was not in imminent danger. Or he could just set under a tree in the heat of a late summer's afternoon and let his mind and eye wander at will. For the Kansas boy who had been behind a plow for well nigh a half century, it seemed good to have some pondering time.

His acres backed up against the butte which afforded good protection for livestock, a real bonus, he figured, in a land where the winds could be unrelenting in their fury. Behind the two-room cabin, some one, years ago, had dug out a sizeable cave in the hillside. It may have once served as temporary shelter for some homesteader or makeshift protection for stock against the winter's cold. Arthur found it to be ideal for the storage of vegetables. The cabin got a tenant and Arthur some company when a bachelor inquired about renting it for a while. He was low on money, but it didn't take much to stir Arthur's sympathetic nature. He had lived long enough himself on the ragged edge of need. Besides, he figured that the cabin was better off occupied than left vacant. The fellow proved to be a quiet and reliable type who took good care of his living quarters.

Marilyn made friends easily and enjoyed her years at Belt high. Her folks weren't keen about riding into Great Falls, but occasionally yielded to her urging and made the trip. Montana's largest city seemed to have it all, especially for the young at heart—the shopping center and theaters, the weekend crowds, the whine of motorcycles, the noise of the big silver birds overhead. Then one May, it was graduation time when the last of the Henderson children would leave the nest. That fall of 1958, Marilyn enrolled in Eastern Montana College in Billings. After one year she took a job in Great Falls and there met a young man from the air base. In due time, she and Harvey Miller were talking marriage. The happy occasion came on February 3, 1961, and made final Arthur's and Lulu's new place in life. For the first time in forty years, they were alone. It would take a while not to listen for footsteps at the front door or to pass Marilyn's vacant bedroom without a haunting loneliness. Now was the time for growing old together, to discover in what ways, as the poetess said, the best was yet to come.

Visits and letters eased the pain of transition. There were trips to the ranch to see Bob and family while Luella's children from Great Falls could always be counted upon to enliven the Henderson home. Along with the oldest who was nearing her teens, there were twin boys and a one-year-old. Other visitors included Amy's son, Richard, who also settled in Great Falls after the war. His boys seemed to have a particular knack for keeping things lively for Uncle Arthur.

Letters from Joyce sometimes left Arthur and Lulu wondering about the difficulties of raising a family when you were moved around so much. Arthur's experience with army life colored his views considerably, though he was prepared to admit that conditions could have improved a lot since 1918. When word came that Joyce's husband was being stationed in Hawaii, the folks decided that at the first opportunity they would go and see for themselves what army life was like.

During the summer of 1964, Arthur's youngest brother, Harold, suffered a fatal heart attack. He had made it through two wars and was working a small farm in Missouri. Only 52, his death was entirely unexpected. Ab and Mame had lived into the eighties and longevity seemed to be in the Henderson blood. But one evening he walked into the house and just slumped to the floor. Arthur and Lulu, at last free to travel, took a plane back for his funeral. Along with the sadness, there was the opportunity to renew contacts with Kansas relatives.

That was in July, and just one year later the phone rang in Belt to bring a new burden of grief. Unbelievingly, Lulu heard the words, "Luella is dead!" Suddenly, tragically, she was gone—not taken in illness but in the seeming bloom of health. As with Roba Mary, Arthur and Lulu struggled with the anguish of "why?" Three times now with their children they had been faced with separation. Only in faith, through the pain, could they believe that it was not eternal. From Lulu's Methodist background came a bit of assurance in the familiar words of Brother Van's "song":

Over and over, yes deeper and deeper,
My heart is pierced through with life's sorrowing cry,
But the tears of the sower and the songs of the reaper
Shall mingle together in joy by and by.

Joyce wrote from Hawaii urging them to come for a visit, to get away for a change and to see the beauty of the Pacific paradise. Also, there was a numerous brood they had not met, and she guaranteed that her ten children would help them forget their grief. Arthur doubted that there was any place better than Montana for climate and scenery, but seeing the family would be great. It took a bit of deciding for they stayed close to their little place in Belt, but one day, in late summer, they packed up and enplaned from Great Falls. Changing planes at Seattle, they found themselves on a huge jet that held 300 passengers or more. Arthur eyed the spacious interior and allowed that there was enough room for a good sized garden. The big bird sailed noiselessly and effortlessly above the clouds. Pretty stewardesses dressed Hawaiian style caught the old homesteader's attention as they served meals and beverages and handed out pillows to cradle your head in pure comfort. Things, he reflected, sure had changed since that first trip to Montana, in the rattling, smelly railroad car. For much of his earlier life, 50 miles on horseback had been considered a good day's ride. Now each hour brought them upwards to 600 miles closer to their destination. His lifetime had spanned a real revolution in transportation.

His various reveries were interrupted by the announcement to fasten seat belts for the approach to Honolulu. Looking out of the window for his first glimpse of Oahu, Arthur had to admit to Lulu that there was something spectacular about Diamond Head. Sitting on the rim of an extinct volcano, it accentuated the Honolulu skyline and seemed to greet visitors from the mainland. In the days that followed, Joyce saw to it that her folks took in most of the sights. On famed Waikiki Beach, Arthur was not unaware of its shapely, bronzed bathers as he fingered the white sand and allowed that it was just about right for mixing cement for various farm projects.

Honolulu's towering hotels gave him a crick in the neck, and he was content to tag along while Joyce and Lulu did their window shopping. He noted with interest that there were large shopping malls much like the better ones in Great Falls. Most memorable was the visit to Pearl Harbor where the old soldier stood in silence over the remains of the *Arizona*. If only, he thought, nations would learn from the tragedy of war. Visits to Sea Life Park to watch reef fish and trained whales were especially interesting to the two Montanans, along with the rides around the island.

The outer islands, they learned, were equally rich in contrasts and varied beauty—more picture-book beaches and cliff-edged shorelines, steep-walled valleys and ranch and croplands, lush vegetation, and barren volcanoes, and everywhere, it seemed, brightly blooming flowers as final testimony to nature's extravagance in this place. Arthur and Lulu heard, too, the stories and legends intended for tourists of how the first inhabitants had come in from the empty sea perhaps a thousand years ago. The English mariner Cook was the first from the western world in 1778 and he called his discovery the Sandwich Islands in honor of a titled countryman. The fabled Kamehameha the Great, giant king of Hawaii, in 1795 hurled warring rivals into the sea and united the islands under his enlightened rule. His descendants held sway until Kamehameha V died without heir in 1872. The last ruling monarch was 300-pound Queen Liliuokalani, who lost her throne in an American-influenced revolt in 1893. Five years later, the islands were annexed by the United States.

Lulu would have lingered longer, but Arthur figured that two weeks was a good visit with Joyce and her family, and that they had seen enough of the sights. He had watched the hula girls perform, learned more about sugar cane and pineapples, and had even driven out to see a herd of white-face cattle that he would have liked to have on his own ranch. Now it was time to get home and prepare for winter. He really didn't have much to look after on the place in Belt, but his life was still tuned to the seasons. The Hawaiian interlude, however, would provide enjoyable memories and stories for years to come.

Back in Belt, Arthur drove over to the ranch to discuss with Bob a matter that he had been considering for some time. They needed more adequate storage facilities to be able to hold grain until the market was right. It would mean thousands of additional dollars for operations or in the bank. Bob had no argument with his father's thinking and soon they had invested in two metal grainaries which increased their storage capacities by some 9000 bushels.

That was step one. Step two was to build a good machine shop. Arthur had always wanted a warm place to work on tractors, trucks, combines, and the like, but he had never had the means. Cold weather made repairs an unpleasant business, and he had had his share of frosted fingers. A good shop was really a necessity for a successful ranch operation and he intended that Bob should have one. The younger Henderson was both surprised and pleased by his father's further plans to improve ranch operations. As for the building, they agreed on a steel structure on cement footings. Arthur left the matter of equipment for Bob's selection. He was more up-to-date on tools and machinery and would be the one using them. With the improvements made, Arthur felt better about leaving all responsibilities for the ranch in his son's hands.

After Hawaii, Arthur and Lulu generally stayed close to Belt. Even the trips to the ranch were spaced further apart. He figured that their children knew where they were and would have to do the traveling now. He was up in his seventies and still had energies for keeping the place in suitable shape, but he cared little for traveling around. Lulu kept busy with housework and quilting and contacts in town. But as October of 1970 came around, Arthur surmised that something special was being planned. Lulu had bought a new dress and given the house an especially thorough cleaning. She had had him mow and trim carefully outside and then suggested that he needed a haircut. But the clincher came when Marilyn arrived home. Lulu was in cahoots with the children in planning a 50th wedding anniversary on October 9th.

The big day came as one of Montana's best, with a warm sun tempered by a touch of autumn's invigorating air. As usual, Arthur was up with the birds, to get his chores done before breakfast. He was under orders from Lulu to be out of his overalls before the guests arrived. But Lulu's sister, Edith and husband, Bill Tanner, came early to help with unfinished tasks and to get the celebration started pioneer style. There was no point in wasting daylight hours.

Bill was the kind that made a gathering go. His natural exuberance and wealth of stories from an uncommonly adventuresome life kept things from getting dull. Roustabout, sailor, cowboy, aviator, gambler—there was little he hadn't tried. Born in Illinois, he and older brother, John, had come to the Geraldine and Square Butte area to live with uncles in 1914. His senior year of high school was spent in Idaho, where he made lasting friendships with Indians on a nearby reservation. 1919 found him on a navy destroyer detailed to mine sweeping. One damaged his ship and Bill got to spend some time in Sweden where he injured a knee playing football while adding to a widening circle of friendships.

Back in Geraldine, he and brother, John, leased some land from their uncle, and then purchased a place northwest of Square Butte. He made a further commitment to the settled life when he married Edith in October of 1926. In addition to raising wheat, cows, and a family, the brothers worked a granite quarry on the ranch. They made time, however, for hunting in the Rockies and fishing on Shoshone Lake in Yellowstone Park.

The itch for adventure brought the purchase of a second-hand plane in 1934. From then on, Bill was earthbound no more either in activity or talk. His Curtis Robin was the only plane in the area for quite some while, but later Geraldine became one of the most air-minded places anywhere. Bill traded for a Piper Cub and the sight of it struck terror into coyote hearts for miles around. Once when a trail derailed near Geraldine, Bill provided the first air ambulance to the hospital in Lewistown. In cars, his fancy ran to compacts and especially the Volkswagon bug. In recent years, Bill and Edith had been spending most of their winters in Las Vegas where he could indulge his liking for bingo and keno.

The house and lawn were soon filled with friends and relatives like Bill and Edith who could share with the Hendersons the memories of 50 years. Many had walked the same road of meager homestead beginnings, betting their futures on a piece of land, often seeing their hopes for the harvest disappear in dust or the fury of a hail storm, in quiet grief burying loved ones taken early in life, yet nuturing an inner strength that somehow outlasted the tragedies and failures. Near the end of the day, they were well seasoned by times good and bad and unshaken in their faith in their land and in their God. Their heritage, they believed, was a goodly one for the numerous children and grandchildren and even great-grandchildren who added to the noisy gathering.

Arrangements had been made for a reception in the Methodist Fellowship Hall. Following a potluck dinner, all eyes focused on an artistically decorated cake—symbol of the couples' fifty years together. Arthur was never one for speeches, but as he and Lulu held the knife nervously on the snow white icing decked with gold, he looked around the crowded room and said simply: "The past fifty years have not always been easy, but they were filled with a wealth no amount of gold can buy." Their eyes met, reflecting the excitement of the moment, and then trembling fingers pressed the knife deep into the cake, triggering cheers of congratulations.

Some people had driven in from distant towns, fourteen came from Great Falls, thirty-two from Geraldine, along with sixty-five from Belt. It was impressive testimony to friendship and love given and received over the years. But at the end of a memorable day, the Hendersons were both emotionally and physically exhausted. Years earlier Arthur could summon up reserve strength. Now, nearing 80, he realized more and more the limits of his endurance. Two very tired but thoroughly happy people gave thanks for the day and their half-century together. Lulu still had some talk left when Arthur rolled over and went to sleep.

Arthur had pretty much given up on any more travel when word came from Kansas in February, 1971, that Claude was terminally ill. The two brothers had always been close and he knew that he had to see Claude again. So, he and Lulu made the trip. Claude was barely conscious when Arthur reached his bedside. Opening his eyes, he lifted a frail hand and whispered, "Arthur, I've been waiting for you to come." Gently the older brother held his hand in a long moment that required no words to token deep and abiding affection.

Arthur mumbled something reassuring about Claude's strength and stout constitution and how he could always lift more hay and best him in a wrestling match. Claude managed a faint smile and whispered that that was long ago. Then—"I knew you'd come. That's why I hung on. I had to see you once more before I die." His grip weakened and his hand dropped as he added, "I'm glad you made it." There was little more to say as Claude's life ebbed and he slept. The next day he was gone.

On the way home, after the funeral, Arthur was quiet and reflective. His thoughts ran through the early days, the good times in a large family on the Kansas frontier, the long hard days of summer getting in the hay, thirsting for a cool drink, falling bone-weary into bed—but also the fishing trips with father and brothers or tracking rabbits on a late fall day across a frozen field. It was so long ago and yet so much a part of what he still held dear. With each passing the curtain seemed to be closing on those distant scenes. Reluctantly he accepted time's decree. With him, only Cecil and Harley and Bertha remained. And she was in poor health in a Benton nursing home.

Thoughts of Cecil brightened Arthur's mood, for his younger brother had promised another visit to Montana. He came with a son to do the driving not long thereafter, and the two old homesteaders made the most of their time together. The cabins they had built were long since gone, but they walked their one-time claims and recalled events deeply etched for them in the soil. Montana had never completely lost its hold on Cecil, and he affectionately recalled that it was here that he had put away boyish things and became a man.

During one of their numerous conversations, they sat on the porch in comfortable rocking chairs waiting for Lulu to put the final touches on the evening meal. Talk drifted naturally to the Great War, as their generation would always call it. Arthur was curious about what "hell-raising" his younger brother might have done. Cecil thought for a bit, and then chuckled: "You remember we used to call the Frenchmen 'Frogs'." Arthur nodded. "Well, some of the fellas found red raspberries. They wouldn't say in whose berry patch. Of course, they weren't any good without milk. So we found a Frog's dairy herd and filled a pail with the strictly fresh stuff. I've always wondered what the Frog thought when he tried to milk his cow that night!"

"How come you didn't hang around to see who did the milking? Could have been his daughter. And some of those French girls weren't hard to look at!"

Cecil ruminated on that lost opportunity and then turned the question of "hell-raising" on his brother. Arthur allowed that he hadn't Cecil's talent for smelling out trouble, but he did recall a fracus or two with the local citizenry.

Changing the subject, Cecil wanted to know why Arthur had never gotten a medal. He had been in the thick of the Argonne business, killed a couple of the enemy, and taken some prisoners.

"I never asked for one," Arthur declared. "I didn't really do anything that brave. The fellas I shot couldn't see me, and the prisoners had no choice. I had the drop on them."

"You should have gotten a medal anyway," Cecil insisted. "Maybe so," Arthur grunted as he rocked his chair back and propped his feet on the porch rail. "Medals didn't seem that important to me. All I wanted to do was come home."

"You and me both," the younger brother agreed. "I think most of the fellas who had been in the thick of action for as long as we were wanted to leave the whole thing behind and forget it.".

Lulu interrupted the old soldiers with a welcome call to supper. "Come on,"Arthur grinned. "Let's see if the women can cook any better than we could." Cecil snickered as he remembered the spartan fare of homestead days and quipped: "They wouldn't have to be very good to beat you with your biscuits and beans!"

All too soon the day came to load the car and head back for Kansas. Arthur hated to see Cecil go. It had been so good talking over old times and just enjoying each other's company. Cecil had always been fun to have around and, though he had sobered and settled with age, his delight in a good story was undiminished with the years. Arthur was quiet by temperament and a good audience for his brother's seemingly endless anecdotes and recollections. Neither Henderson had a dry eye as they said goodbye, not knowing when, if ever, they would be together again.

Visits from the children and grandchildren usually made the day. During the summer, the grandchildren could help Arthur gather vegetables from the garden or see what ripe pleasures might be sampled from Lulu's berry patch. The Hendersons always lived simply and not let a concern for things get in the way of enjoying their children. Crayon marks could be cleaned from the wall and jelly from the floor. Household items could be replaced or repaired that had fallen victim to childish play. Time was too important to fuss over things when all too soon children would be grown up and gone and the days with grandchildren would be too few and far between.

From time to time, Bob dropped by to discuss ranch affairs. The operation now included 1760 acres, of which 700 acres were in wheat and barley. He was farming half summer fallow and half crop and also running 30 head or so of cows. Yields per acre continued to rise with the use of soil conservation measures and chemical sprays now applied by airplanes. The mid-seventies were proving to be particularly good for the wheat producers, with favorable market conditions and high prices. Arthur rejoiced with Bob in the good times, but cautioned him, in the perspective of his experience, that drought would come again, markets deteriorate, and prices would fall. Still, it was quite a different world than the one he had first known—of isolated homesteads dotting a barren landscape, where families barely existed on 320 acres and hoped for better times. The elder Henderson was always pleased when Bob sought his advice, which usually proved to be sound.

Joyce's husband had retired from the navy and taken up religious work. That had always been an ambition and he was now located in a church. The death of their eleventh child was also a factor in his decision and a sorrow that Joyce carried with her. Somehow she blamed herself and could not resolve her remorse. The fact that her ten children were strong and healthy only seemed to accentuate the tragedy of the little one who had been snatched away.

On a visit home, she sought help from her parents, knowing that they had also suffered loss. Arthur was not one to talk much about religion, but on this occasion, he shared with his daughter the faith that had always anchored his family. Mame especially had radiated a belief in the Eternal Goodness that enabled her to bury two children and see three sons go off to war. Each evening, he remembered, when the house was quiet, she would go alone into the kitchen and, kneeling by a chair, present her problems to her Lord. Not all for which she prayed was granted. Sometimes the cup could not pass. Sometimes faith meant acceptance, for by the very terms of life the outcome of the harvest was in other hands. But from this habit of prayer came a spirit of calm trust. And her example, Arthur said quietly, had helped him through his own dark hours, and was a blessing he would never forget.

For Joyce, there was healing in such sharing and assurance in knowing that she belonged to a family where others had endured loss and found strength through faith to take up life again.

Late in the decade, the other surviving brother came for a visit. Harley was the third from youngest and the one who had answered Mame's hope for a minister in the family. Slight of build, like Arthur, Harley had graduated from Ottawa University and received his divinity degree from Colgate Rochester in 1936. An ordained Baptist preacher, he had combined a career of preaching and teaching, and also did some writing. Still a child when Arthur left home, he had not seen much of his older brother. The trip from his home in Cheyenne was an opportunity to see Arthur again and to learn more about his life as a homesteader and wheat farmer.

Arthur was now in his upper eighties, with poor hearing and faltering memory. But with Lulu's assistance, he could piece together most of the past, and his story was one Harley felt needed to be recorded. Few were remaining from that last great migration west to the Montana homestead frontier. He was one who had stayed when drought withered the promised land, put deep roots in the soil, and became a proud citizen of his adopted state. Never, he recalled, had he given serious consideration of going back to Kansas. In the rolling lands of Geraldine country, he had found home.

124

EPILOGUE

Little did Arthur and Lulu suspect when they celebrated 50 years together that there would be another such occasion ten years later. But on Sunday, October 12, 1980, about 250 relatives and friends assembled at the Belt School Cafeteria to honor them on their 60th wedding anniversary. The children and numerous grandchildren came in from around Montana, California, and South Dakota. Sister Edith and husband Billy were back again and Harley was there from Cheyenne to invoke God's blessing on the occasion. Regretfully, Cecil was unable to come but vowed he would see Arthur again.

The tables were festive with flowers and once more Arthur and Lulu had a beautifully decorated cake to cut. A scrapbook was presented commemorating their long life together. But most of all, there was the ever-rich experience of renewing acquaintances, reviving memories, and being reassured in the warmth of friendship of the wisdom of Arthur's Montana passage.

As Arthur crossed over his 90th year, he still kept up his daily round of chores, started according to long custom before breakfast, working in the garden, irrigating the place, puttering with this and that, but finding more time to sit in his favorite chair beneath the tree in the back yard, remembering the past as he sipped lemonade on a hot August afternoon. Nearby an old tractor rusted with the seasons, symbolizing his long tutelage to the soil. Like him, its last harvest was in. Overalls hung loosely on a slight frame that once had wrestled rocks and guided an unruly plow through stubborn homestead soil. Poor hearing barred much of a conversation, but the faded blue eyes in a face textured by sun and wind signaled a lively interest that belied the years. Fingering the soiled Certificate of Honorable Discharge and chuckling over his Company's picture, he remembered how his buddies had called him "Henny," and how once he could name them all. He recollected, too, how his Montana adventure had begun on that day in Fort Benton. "Lord," he exclaimed, "it was cold."

Lulu, younger by several years, kept busy with hobbies like quilting and with activities in the church and in town. The soft brown eyes that once captured the bachelor homesteader conveyed a warm welcome to visitors and the openhanded hospitality she had practiced since pioneer days. Among the changes they had seen, Arthur was most impressed with the transformation in agriculture, unparalleled in the history of the world. In Ab's day, he reflected, a farmer hoped to feed his family and market enough to provide clothes and shelter. Now, with much less acreage, the farmer was producing enough food to feed 75 people besides himself. Lulu added her observations about the modern age of convenience, the miracles in transportation and communication, but wondered about the human costs in the loss of close family ties and the neighborliness of earlier times.

In the fullness of years, they still live by the wisdom of pioneer times, taking each day as it comes, knowing that along with the hardships and grief they have seen, there have been the compensating blessings of a lifetime together and something of accomplishment in their hard work on a very small bit of God's good earth.